Come As You Are

Come As You Are

CLASSbooks

Classeminars, Inc.
P.O. Box 36551
Alburquerque, NM 87176

Printed in the USA
Cover and Interior Design by *k*ae Creative Solutions
Editing Dr. Edna Ellison
Cover photograph by Louise Roach/Dreamstime.com

Classbooks, Inc.
P.O. Box 36551
Albuquerque, NM 87176

Published in association with
Bold Vision Books
PO Box 2011
Friendswood, Texas 77549

For information on Bible versions, see page 185

Table of Contents

Introduction

E ver wish you could be a great writer? Do the If only's of life stop you? "If only I had studied harder in school. . ." "If only I had lived a pure life." "If only I were better at grammar." "If only my family had encouraged me more." "If only my past were not so rotten and evil!"

"I'm not good enough."

Ever want to be a confident Christian, maybe a future evangelist or a powerful Bible teacher, if only the past were not still standing in your way? You may have thought, "Surely God can't use me." It's true that all of us are guilty of sin (mistakes, failures, falling short of our good goals, wickedness, doing bad things to hurt others). Paul says all of us have sinned and missed the mark of perfection. (See Romans 3:23)

Come As You Are brings good news: Nothing you can do will ever make God stop loving you.

This book focuses on one main idea: Because of His unbelievable, abundant love, you can come into the presence of Jesus just as you are. Between the pages of this book, you will find writers who have expressed in a unique way how they have come to a moment of truth that changed them forever. Each of these moments of truth is like a fulcrum point, like a long lever, a turning point, from which they can move the world. Authors of this book have found a fantastic, overall truth: They don't have to run or hide from God anymore. They can believe that God's love is so vast that He covers us with compassion, understanding and forgiveness.

This book is our gift to you, our reader. We pray you will relish each true story and celebrate the victories of the authors as you get to know each of them better. God bless you as you grow in Him through the experiences, prayers, and miracles of others.

White Gloves or Not?

Linda Gilden

I pulled my little blue suitcase from under the bed and opened it. I put the important things in first: "Sweet Doggie" (my shaggy, stuffed nighttime cuddle dog), peppermint candy, and the camera Mama and Daddy had given me for my birthday. Then I took the small pile of things Mama had folded and put them on top. Tomorrow seemed a long way away.

I had never been on an airplane before and woke up on departure day so excited I couldn't sit still. I put on my Sunday dress Mama had ironed so carefully. My coat and white gloves were on the table by the door. Bebo, my grandmother who was taking me to New York, suggested I wear my Easter hat as well but eventually gave in to my protests on that!

When we got to the airport I saw people dressed in all kinds of finery. The wide hallways, constant announcements, and frequent roar of airplane engines kept me engrossed. And when we boarded the plane, it looked more like a big group of folks headed to Sunday school than travelers headed to various destinations.

Times have really changed. Recently as I traveled and observed those traveling with me, it appeared as if they had "come as you are" stamped on their boarding passes.

Heading to security, I followed "Stylish Susan." Despite the struggle of trying to walk in six-inch heels on a brick and mortar hallway, she was determined to travel in those shoes. Between the shoes and the heavy bags on her shoulders, the straight line to security became a zig-zagging path.

From there to the boarding gate, Sleepy Sam was in front of me. His hair was a mess, his shoulders slumped, and it looked as if he had slept in his clothes so he could sleep until the very last minute.

As I sat at the gate for several hours, many other travelers passed by. When I heard a rapid, steady tap-tap rhythm on the floor, I knew Late Larry must be on the way. His gate waiting area was empty and he never slowed until he was through the boarding door.

Then there was Fit Frances. She had discovered a few spare minutes before boarding so she was taking a quick walk around the concourse. She obviously planned for this exercise because she was wearing her sweats.

Yes, things have changed since I took that first flight in my church duds. But things have changed at church as well.

I grew up in the era where you didn't cross the threshold of the church unless you were properly dressed complete with white gloves. Social rules have changed to a "come as you are" mentality. Many people who come to church on Sunday look just like airport people!

I distinctly remember when I discovered God had an open-door policy for me to come to Him as I was, no matter what. His love just cut right through my outer covering and went straight to my heart. From that moment I was the keeper of His holy temple and did my best to make it look nice. But He spoke clearly to my heart and told me it was okay to leave the white gloves at home. *What's important is that people see what is on the inside and that My love overflow from you to every person you meet.*

Next time I go to the airport, I think I will cut Susan, Larry, Sam, and Frances a little slack. Their "temple" may not look anything like mine, but underneath their stiletto heels and the fitness clothes, is another brother or sister whom God loves just as He loves me.

Prayer: Lord, Why is it so hard for us to realize that we don't have to change anything for you to love us? Why do we think we have to make everything right before we ask for your forgiveness and acceptance? Bless this reader and fill him or her with your love and the realization that You love him just the way he is. Amen.

 ⫷

Linda Gilden is an author, speaker, editor, ghostwriter, and writing coach. Author of over a thousand articles and eight books including *Called to Write,* she directs the CLASS and Carolina Christian Writers Conferences. Linda lives in SC with her family– a great source of speaking and writing material! www.lindagilden.com

Come As You Are

Gerry Wakeland

For I am convinced that neither death, nor life, nor angels, nor rulers, nor things present, nor things to come, nor powers, nor height, nor depth, nor anything else in all creation, will be able to separate us from the love of God in Christ Jesus our Lord (Romans 8:38 NRSV).

Guilt and shame are two of the cruelest tools that the enemy uses to drive a wedge between us and the Father. I know this from personal experience. I was the victim of these tools for years.

My earthly father, my daddy, was killed tragically in 1968 when our home caught fire and he was trapped inside. At the time of the fire, my 11-year-old sister was in her bedroom. Before he succumbed to the toxic fumes, my father managed to yell at her to get out of the house. She ran through the front door into the yard, where we found her when my mother and I arrived home a short time later.

Our old farmhouse was already engulfed in flames and my mother drove as fast as she could to the nearby neighbors to use the phone to call the fire department. By the time they arrived it was too late.

Nothing could be done. Everything was lost, even my daddy.

As I sat in the back of the car the sun began to set and the cold winter day became colder. But colder still was the feeling that swept over me, the feeling of guilt. As darkness settled over a scene that consisted of a few fire fighters guarding a pile of embers, my mother insisted I put on my coat. The coat I chose to wear that day was not made of wool or fleece but rather the coat of responsibility and I wore that coat for years until it was tattered and threadbare.

Why the feelings of guilt, you ask? We should have been home, my mother and I. If we had been home this would not have happened. But instead we had spent the entire day waiting to see an orthopedic surgeon about my knee, a surgeon that had never shown up. Oh, he had his reasons and they were all good, but at that moment in time I knew that it was because of me that we were not home to prevent this catastrophe.

As I crawled into a strange bed that night and lay my head on a strange pillow I was sure that God no longer loved me. My daddy was dead and it was all my fault.

Months of counseling later, nothing had changed. I still felt responsible and held onto the guilt and shame that went along with that responsibility. It controlled my life. It affected my relationship with my mother, my sister and my friends. It impacted my school work. I became moody and even more introverted than normal. Most of all it created a huge chasm between me and God.

Months passed and then years. I found myself desperately seeking the love that was lost that day, the love of two fathers. But nothing could fill the hole in my heart or the hole in my soul. I floundered through life still seeking, still longing, but not finding any answers.

Then one very late night in 1988 God finally managed to get through to me, to convince me that He had not forgotten me at all and prove to me that He still loved me. He always had. But even after experiencing reconciliation with Father God I still struggled with the guilt of my daddy's death.

In the spring of 1995 our Women's Ministry Director invited me to attend a women's retreat in Asilomar, CA. It was a beautiful retreat center right along the Pacific Ocean and it was an incredible time of healing in my life.

On Saturday night the retreat leader, following the leading of the Holy Spirit, offered an unscheduled late night session on emotional healing. She took a small group of us through a visual exercise that allowed me to let go of all the guilt and shame I had carried for so long. It convinced me that *nothing can separate me from God's love.*

This is true for us all. No matter who we are or what we have done, God does, and always will, love us. He is our Father. Take ownership of that. Choose to wear that coat with dignity and pride.

Prayer: Father, there are many who are burdened by the guilt and shame of circumstances in their lives. I pray that you would provide an opportunity for their healing so that the torment they suffer would be resolved. Amen.

◈

Gerry Wakeland is the President of CLASSEMINARS, Inc. She resides in Albuquerque, NM where she also serves on the staff of Albuquerque's First Baptist Church. She is the mother of two amazing daughters and grandmother to four rambunctious grandsons.

Is My Baby Alive?

Beth Patch

Five months pregnant was beyond the danger point of another miscarriage, I thought. But that January morning a crimson puddle appeared where I sat in shock.

Fighting back tears, I asked the emergency room doctor, "Is my baby still alive? I haven't felt him move all day."

"I'm sorry," he answered. "We don't have obstetric capabilities at this hospital. I've called for an ambulance to take you to one which does."

"How long before they get here?" I asked.

"Probably an hour."

The white sheets on the narrow bed provided little warmth and I never before felt so alone and scared.

"Don't be anxious or think the worst," I told myself. "Don't cry. It will stress your body." I remained still and so did my womb.

My baby's chance for survival rested solely on the awaited medical team. One hour became two, then three.

"Your transport is here." The doctor drew back the curtain. Two men wearing paramedic jackets helped hoist me to my chariot of hope.

Cold snowflakes fell on my face as they rolled me out and hurriedly across the parking lot.

"Why were we going through the parking lot to get to their ambulance?" my mind wondered. "And why hadn't they checked for my baby's heartbeat?"

My mouth remained closed. My eyes focused on my would-be heroes. One was stocky, in his 30s, with curly black hair poking through his hat. The other was a younger man, thin and tall with soft brown eyes.

"Lift her up, nice and easy," the burly man said, as they positioned my gurney in the back of their white van. "That's it."

He went around to the driver's seat as the younger one took a seat beside me. My eyes surveyed my special capsule of care: an aluminum cavern with bare walls and the hollow sound of emptiness. The EMT badge on the young man's shirt was the only medical-looking clue.

"We should be there in about 45 minutes," the driver called out to the air.

My eyes fastened on my seated companion, "If I should go into labor while we are on the way to this hospital, what do you have in here to help me?"

"We have some sheets and towels up there," he said confidently as he motioned to the white cabinets anchored above my head.

I glanced up, swallowed hard, and tears began streaming down the sides of my face. My baby's life was still an unknown and I lay in the back of a work van, traveling the streets of New Jersey in a snowstorm. I had valiantly waited for this? I could feel my heart beating in my state of silent mourning and longed for some indication of another heartbeat in my womb.

"Oh, God!" My sob pierced the silence. "I see whose hands this is in!"

As I began to acknowledge his power, my soul felt the need to confess my sins to God before asking for His help. "Please forgive me, Jesus. I have walked away from You and done things my own way for so long."

For the next twenty minutes, I confessed every sin I could remember, out loud, as if Jesus and I were the only ones in the van (more information than my chaperones ever expected).

"I don't want to stray any more. I know You are in control of all things," I confirmed.

Then I begged and pleaded many times and ways, "Please save my baby, Lord; let him live! Please give me a sign that there's still life in there."

"Five minutes to the hospital," the driver announced.

I kept praying and pleading. Then God answered as only He can do.

"The baby kicked!" I screamed. "He kicked! He's alive! O, Jesus, thank You!"

My tears flowed like a river. My mouth could only say, "Thank You, Jesus," over and over.

As the men rolled me out of the now-worship-van, even the burly man's eyes filled with tears.

God met us on the snowy ride through New Jersey. My baby's survival had been in His hands all along—our true rescue and salvation.

For reflection: What do you need to turn over to the trust of God alone?

Prayer: Father God, You promise never to leave us or forsake us and we are often the ones who have left You. Thank You for Your never-ending grace that always meets us right where we are. Help us to seek You first in all things, as You are the only one who gives us true hope. Amen.

Beth Patch is a freelance writer and an editor/Internet producer for CBN.com. She's a frequent staff member/workshop leader at Christian writers conferences. Beth's favorite blessings are her husband, children, and grandchildren.

Don't Duck the Darkness

Gloria Penwell

Yea, though I walk through the valley of the shadow of death
I will fear no evil, for thou art with me…
Psalm 23::4 ESV

All right, listen up. I want all cell phones, cameras, and flashlights put in the basket. Get in line, and grab the hand of the person in front of you and the person behind you. There will be no talking whatsoever. Follow me," shouted the camp counselor.

As we stumbled in the darkness down the path to the woods, I could feel the clammy hand of the sixth-grade boy in front of me begin to tremble. I squeezed his hand, trying to reassure him and hoping mine wasn't trembling as well. We tripped along, stubbing toes on tree roots or an occasional stone. Why were we here? Slowly, we began to hear sounds that were not our own. A tree frog here, a bird song there. And wonder of wonders, we started to see the faint lights of the moon, stars, and fireflies through the tree branches. We were learning to be still, to listen, and to really see.

No one likes to walk in darkness. When bad times come, we tend to want to skip them and get on to the good times.

As humans we don't choose to go through tough things. We wonder why God allows them to happen to us. Philippians 4:4 says, "Rejoice in the Lord always, and again I say rejoice" (KJV). That perplexes me. People suffer with medical crisis for themselves or their loved ones, a child or spouse dies, a teen makes wrong choices, and a family member loses a job or income. Are we supposed to rejoice in these dark places? Thank God for them? How can I see God's hand in the midst of such trials? If my heart is breaking, how can I rejoice in this place? That doesn't seem right. What possible good can come from this? We want the rosy path; the life without trials.

We live in a country where we are taught and admired for our self-sufficiency. The problem comes when we're dealing with God and he wants to direct our lives.

I wish we could always know what the big lesson is when we lean into the Lord during our suffering, but that's not true. Sometimes the only lesson learned is that our Father loves us, and ultimately that's enough. Trusting Him and giving thanks in all things brings us with open hands before his throne. When I am broken and have nothing, then God is able to do things in my life.

C.S. Lewis once said, "I know now, Lord, why you utter no answer. You yourself are the answer. Before your face questions die away."

During the darkness I need to grasp God's hand, be still, and listen for his voice.

Prayer: Dear Lord, please lead me through the dark times in my life. Help me to trust you and be still and listen to your voice. Thank you for the hard things as well as the joyous things that come my way. Help me to see you in all things. Amen.

∾

Gloria Penwell traveled for many years with her husband, Dan Penwell, attending numerous writers' conferences and conventions. Since Dan's death in 2010 she has been attending several conferences a year where she teaches, interviews authors for AMG Publishers, and mentors new writers. She is assistant director of the CLASS Christian Writers Conference in Albuquerque, NM, and a member of the board of CLASSeminars.

Our Uniqueness

Florence Littauer

God did not make us all alike. Each one of us is unique. Paul tells us that we should examine ourselves and find out what gifts God has given us and what weaknesses He wishes us to overcome with our willingness and His power. Paul compares us to a body where Christ is the head and we are the parts.

Under his control all the different parts of the body fit together, and the whole body is held together by every joint with which it is provided. So when each separate part works as it should, the whole body grows and builds itself up through love (Ephesians 4:16 GNB)

God made each one of us different, so we could function in our own role. He made some of us to be *feet* – to move, to administer, to accomplish, like Powerful Choleric. He made some of us to be *minds* – to think deeply, to feel, to write, like Perectly Melancholy. He made some of us to be *hands* – to serve, to smooth, to soothe, like Peaceful Phlegmatic. He made some of us to be *mouths* – to talk, to teach, to encourage, like Popular Sanguine.

Now hath God set the members, every one of them in the body, as it hath pleased him (1 Corinthians 12:18 HCSB).

God could have made us all Popular Sanguines. We would have lots of fun but accomplish little.

He could have made us all Perfect Melancholies. We would have been organized and charted but not very cheerful.

He could have made us all Powerful Cholerics. We would have been all set to lead, but impatient that no one would follow.

He could have made us all Peaceful Phlegmatics. We would have had a peaceful world but not much enthusiasm for life.

Prayer: God, you created each of us to fill a specific function in the body of Christ. Help each of us to fulfill our position so we will be unified and the results will be harmonious.

Florence Littauer is an award winning speaker and author with numerous books to her credit. Since its release in 1983, her book *Personality Plus* has sold over a million copies. The personality concepts introduced in this book have changed thousands of lives and saved hundreds of marriages. In the past 30 years, Florence has equipped over 1000 Certified Personality Trainers across the world to share tools that help individuals better understand themselves and others by understanding the personalities.

From *Personality Plus* by Florence Littauer ©1992 by Fleming H. Revell

Loved Anyway

Arlene Sikorski

No one could have felt further away from God than I did.

For the first twenty-five years of my life, I never felt God loved me. I just couldn't seem to get close to Him, no matter how hard I tried. I wanted to believe all the wonderful things I heard about Him in church, but after struggling for years with the question of how a good God could allow all the suffering of this world, I finally rejected Him. I told Him I was done trying to believe He was good. If that meant eternal separation from Him, so be it.

That's how furious I was with Him.

And yet the coldness that came over me right afterwards stunned me. I felt empty. For a few months, I experienced the meaninglessness of life without God but feared that my rejecting Him had made Him turn His back to me forever.

Nevertheless, I went back to church, listened to Christian radio, and tried to pray. I began to feel a glimmer of hope that maybe, just maybe, God could forgive me.

One beautiful September morning as I listened to a radio pastor, he read from Psalm 2: "Why do the heathen rage?"

He paused. I thought, "That's me. I raged against God—against the unfairness of life and all my unanswered questions."

Then he said, "Jesus bore our raging on the cross." And in that instant, the love of God flooded over me in a way I had never known. The glass wall that had always separated me from God shattered, and I was welcomed into His marvelous presence. It was a dramatic, life-changing moment. Since then, although I have failed Him countless times, I know that there is nothing I can do to lose His love.

Even when I was a rebel against God, He was planning a better identity for me: a beloved friend of His. He desired me to become the glorious, beautiful, immortal, loving woman He created me to be. I never will have all the answers to the mysteries and the sufferings of this life. But this I know: God loves me deeply, dearly, unconditionally—more than I could have imagined. Because He is Love and Grace, I can trust Him with my unanswered questions.

Prayer: Thank you, loving Father, for the tender humility you showed and the great grace that you lavished on me, even after I rejected you. Thank you for accepting me just as I am.

&

Arlene Sikorski loves playing piano and guitar, hiking, dancing, and spending time with her nephew and four nieces. She has just completed her first book, *Never Too Late: Stories of Faith, Hope, and Love. Amen.*

Ending Well

Dennis Hensley

When people of destiny die, they are content. They don't say, "If only I had it to do over. I wish I would have _____." Instead, like Jesus, they have their own version of "It is finished." Do you think it was mere "coincidence" Thomas Jefferson and John Adams both died on the fourth of July, 1826, *exactly* one-half century after America had declared independence as a nation? These men died thinking, "We did it! It is accomplished."

Jesus talked in John 16:33 about people being at peace despite the challenges the world would throw at those who choose to follow a righteous cause: "I have told you these things, so that in me you may have peace. In this world you will have trouble. But take heart! I have overcome the world" (KJV).

Is any of this to say you won't be amazed—perhaps even temporarily terrified—over your personal call to destiny? Consider it normal.

Wasn't it Moses who said, "Who am I, Lord, that I should go before Pharoah?"

Didn't Gideon say, "But, Lord, I am from a humble family, in which I, myself, am the humblest?"

Even Isaiah argued, "But, Lord, I am a man of unclean lips."

More often than not, it may be your seeming "weakness" that will make you all the more appealing for God's purpose. When David, a little boy, slew the giant Goliath, it was obvious it was the hand of the Lord at work. The apostle Paul noted, "When I am weak, that's when I am strong," meaning the more his corporeal strength failed him, the more he was required to call upon the power of God, which only served to make him more forceful and dynamic than ever.

Prayer: Father, show us our destiny and your will. Then help us reach our purpose with your mighty power. Amen

Dennis E. Hensley holds four university degrees in communication, including a PhD in literature and linguistics. Dr. Hensley is the author of more than fifty books and more than three thousand magazine and newspaper articles, as well as stage plays, film scripts, and songs. He is a professor at Taylor University, where he serves as director of the professional writing major. Dr. Hensley and his wife Rose have two grown, married children and four grandchildren.

Excerpt from *Jesus in the 9 to 5*, by Dennis Hensley © 2013 by AMG Publishers.

He Lifts Me Up

Karen Porter

Behind our house near the fence is a beautiful stand of lilies. They are blooming in red, yellow, purple, and orange. I don't know how they survived. Years ago, we dug them up at Grandmother's house to bring them to our house, but we forgot to plant them for a long time. We finally put them in the flowerbed and they miraculously lived. Later the cows leaned over the fence and chewed them to the ground. Just when they sprang up again, Dad mowed them flat. We've forgotten to water or feed them and now weeds surround them. But there they are—brightly blooming and beautiful. It is as if God reached down and pulled them up to stand straight and glorious.

When my busy, breakneck schedule overwhelms me, I feel as though I've been forgotten or chewed down to the nub. Sometimes hurtful or careless words mow me down. Most often my defeats are because I've blown it, allowing anger, impatience, or unforgiveness to rule my day. The weeds creep in because I've failed to regularly get food and water from God's Word. But even when I am in deep weeds, He reaches down and pulls me up. No matter how far my trouble takes me, I am never out of His reach.

He sees my potential instead of my failures. He reaches down, brings me up, and helps me blossom. When He takes me in His hand, I flourish and thrive.

Psalm 18:16 reminds me that no matter how much trouble I get into, my God of the second chance is ready to rescue me and accept me just as I am.

> He reached down from on high and took hold of me; he drew
> me out of deep waters (Psalm 18:16 NIV).

Prayer: Father, as I evaluate my life, all I see are my failures and mistakes. In those time, help me remember Grandmother's lilies. Amen.

∽

Karen Porter is an author of six books, an international speaker, a successful businesswoman, and coach. Karen is a senior staff member of CLASSEMINARS, Inc. Her latest book *Speak Like Jesus* helps aspiring speakers learn to speak for and like the Master.

Light in This Present Darkness

Jennifer Hoyer

B ang!"

I heard my brother's head smack the carpeted floor. My stepdad dragged him down the hallway and into his bedroom. The door closed behind them. *I can't let this happen to my brother again, I have to do something,* I thought to myself. I told my mother what had happened. A day or two later, we were living in an abuse shelter. This would be the first of three abuse shelters that my mom and the three of us kids would lived in for the next four years of our lives.

Abuse destroyed my family and caused me to go down a path that was so dark it almost stole my life. This abuse caused me to fear and despise men to the point where the only way I felt safe was to be in control of them.

At fifteen, I unknowingly became involved with two men—one whom I had counted as a friend—who were willing and ready to sell me. Knowing I could be killed without their protection, I didn't see another option. I remember going a "friend's" apartment, sitting on his couch, and listening to him talk to another guy about how much money they could sell me for. This night destroyed the last shred of hope and worth I had left in my life.

At that moment I cut off all of my feelings; I couldn't afford to feel anymore. My life was strictly centered around making other people happy. Whatever they wanted, I gave—no matter how grave the cost. The consequences of not complying seemed worse than what I was experiencing. I was locked in a cage of fear which I could not escape. By the end of that year, I had been kicked out of school, put on probation, and made my family miserable.

I was at the end of myself and what I could handle on my own strength. The only shred of light I could see at the end of this dark tunnel was to end my life. I decided to mix a bunch of different chemicals together, lock myself in a bathroom, and fall asleep, never to wake up again. After my suicide attempt failed, I began to spiral downward even faster. My mother didn't know what else to do with me so she decided to send me to Teen Challenge of New Mexico. I could never have begun to imagine the new life that was waiting ahead of me and what it would entail.

When I arrived at Teen Challenge, I was consumed with an overwhelming sense of guilt and pain. I didn't feel I deserved their love, yet it was given to me freely. When I couldn't sleep, they prayed for me. When I hated them, they loved me. When I cried so hard that I was shaking, they were the arms of Jesus holding me close. Through them I learned what God's love looked like. However, a day would come when I truly experienced the love of my Lord in a personal and unforgettable way.

Still, I couldn't handle the guilt of my past anymore. I had been taught that prayer was a powerful tool that could break down any wall. Just as I was—guilty, broken, and misused—I got on my knees before My Lord and asked Him to forgive me and release me from the burdens that I had been chained to for so long. As soon as I began to pray, I felt lighter as God was lifting my burdens. He took away the pain that had been gouged deeply into my heart. Compared to the rest of the people in my life, He was tender and gentle. His love caught me by surprise. I knew at that moment God was the only One I wanted to serve for the rest of my life. People may have come to sell me, but Jesus Christ bought me back from sin.

Beloved, understand that no matter how difficult your situation may be or how unforgivable you think your mistakes are, God will never forsake you. You are never beyond the length His arm can reach.

Prayer: Lord, help me today to understand I cannot handle the pain and guilt of my sin. However, you died on the cross for me—*just as I am*—so that I could be set free from this burden. You are calling me to stand up and fight the good fight of faith. Help me to rely on your strength during this time of testing. Amen

Jennifer Hoyer is a graduate of Teen Challenge of New

Mexico and is now on staff. She is from Indianapolis, Indiana, and has a younger brother and sister. Her life's goal is to become a missionary.

Have You Ever Raised Twins?

Robyn Carrillo

The nurse paraded us into the room and we stood on display before the group. Never had my husband and I stood in such a crowded hospital room. *Aren't there limits to the number of visitors?* I counted twelve people besides the birth mother, my husband, and myself. The newborn twins slept contently in their single bassinet beside the bed.

All eyes glared at us as the birth mother introduced us to her family members and friends. At thirty-five, we were older than everyone except for the birth mother's parents. Two teen girls were obviously pregnant, one wearing regular-sized jeans unbuttoned and unzipped. Nobody smiled. Nobody was happy to see us.

When the questions began I could feel us sliding down the rabbit's hole. "Do you know how to clean the umbilical cords? What are you going to do with them when they fall off? You know it is good luck to save them. How are you going to discipline them? You know if you put shoes on newborns it deforms their feet, right? Do you know formula makes babies throw up? When are you going to have them circumcised? Laughter erupted from the crowd. A rough-looking teenaged boy in the back of the room shouted, "Have you ever raised twins?"

We tried to be pleasant and answer their questions. We were on trial, and this angry crowd was the judge and the jury. The birth mother's mom played the prosecutor asking rapid-fire questions, and then led the laughter if we hesitated or stumbled.

My face and neck flushed and sweat slid down my back. My husband's face was tight with tension. We were trapped. The birth mother had not signed the adoption papers yet, so we didn't want to cause any conflicts. We wanted to make a good impression and prove we were fit parents to adopt her twin baby boys. Only hours old, the twins slept unaware of the verbal tug-of-war going on over them.

As I felt naked and defenseless before these accusers, my ugly pride welled up inside me. I wanted to yell back, "Who are you to question our parenting? We were more qualified than anyone in the room to raise these babies. We were already raising a ten-year-old daughter and an eight-year-old son. We owned a successful business and lived in a large house. We would be able to take these babies on vacations to Hawaii and send them to private school. How dare they belittle us when they didn't even know who we were!

Immediately I was convicted about my pride. I realized I also showed God my pride. I wanted to show Him all the great things I accomplished for Him. I wanted to give Him my list of credentials, my obedience to Him, my service to Him, and my sacrifice to Him. But as it was in that maternity room, all those accomplishments fell to the ground before our Holy God. They didn't mean anything. He did not need my service or sacrifice. My list of spiritual achievements did not impress Him.

Through God's grace and power to move mountains He brought about the adoption of our twins, with nothing we did nor anything we brought with us. We did not earn this blessing because we were good parents. No. God's grace caused it to happen.

Prayer: Lord, thank you that it is by your amazing grace and not our list of accomplishments that you love and accept us. We stand bare before you bringing nothing, and you love us with an everlasting love. Amen.

❧

Living in Albuquerque, NM, **Robyn Carrillo** loves the Lord with all her heart. She is a business owner, Israel tour host, pastor's wife, and Mom to four great kids and two hilarious dogs.

A Beacon of Light

Susan Titus Osborn

Shivering, I zipped my blue windbreaker tightly around my neck. The damp air chilled me as I stood watching the fog roll in. I walked faster along the shore, hoping an increased heart rate would mean greater warmth to my body. Darkness was quickly settling in, but I felt determined to take my nightly walk. This was my quiet time.

The clouds overhead blocked the moon, so I carefully picked my way across the rocky portion of the beach to the sandy stretch. In the distance, I saw the beacon from the lighthouse on the point. I used its flashing light to guide me.

How often my life revolved like that beacon, so busy and yet going nowhere. As a single parent with two sons, I had to work outside of my home. I often felt stress from the many demands on my time.

While I continued walking toward the lighthouse, I stared at the circling light. It took on new significance. Because of one bright light, captains would sail far enough from the shore to avoid crashing on the rocky reefs which jutted out from the point. That lamp warned all the passing ships and guided them to safety.

Watching the revolving beacon, I felt a close identity with it. Many of the people who pass through my life are not Christians. Like the ships, they might steer close to dangerous rocky places. Sometimes they seek advice. Could I set priorities that would influence their lives by the Christian example of my own life? The steadiness of my inner peace and strength come from the Lord. If I share this with them, they may desire to know Him better. At that moment, I determined my goal would be to shed light like the powerful beacon.

What about the example I am setting for my children? Am I so preoccupied with my work that I tune them out when they talk to me? Instead of ignoring them, I should use those precious moments to listen. Our conversations could be channeled to draw our family closer together and nearer to God. I vowed to concentrate on listening more carefully to my children in the future.

Finally, I reached the lighthouse. It was time to turn around and start back. However, I lingered for a moment, gazing up at the powerful light. Grasping its awesome responsibility, I thought of my own. Tomorrow I would try to imitate that beacon, shining brightly to help those who cross my path.

Prayer: Dear Lord, help me to be a shining light to those around me just as that lighthouse beacon is a guiding light for ships. May your light shine through me.

❧

Susan Titus Osborn is the director of the Christian Communicator Manuscript Critique Service. She has authored over 30 books. She lives in Fullerton, California, with her husband Dick. Contact her through her website: www.Christiancommunicator.com/.

Two Choices

Joyce Zook

D id I hear her right? "Tell me again," I said, afraid to trust what I'd heard.

Isolated from any curious eyes, we stood in front of the large bathroom mirror. No one entered the bathroom while my girlfriend told the unbelievable tale of my husband's indiscretions committed with her and others I knew.

Tears blurred my eyes. I felt like screaming, but the sound got stuck in my throat. My thoughts raced, looking for a safe place to land. I struggled to breathe. *How could this happen without my even knowing about it?* In a few seconds, my friend became my enemy. I felt angry, betrayed, and, rejected. Girlfriends I counted on couldn't be trusted any more. I grabbed my purse and raced out the door without saying a word.

My marriage could never be healed, but due to circumstances out of my control, I couldn't leave. We seldom sat in the same room and rarely spoke to each other. I spent my days at the library in an attempt to drown out my raging anger and frustration by escaping into the world of science fiction.

Three months after that fateful night I decided to try a bunch of new activities. I joined a choral society with folks from several military bases and learned the songs for the spring program.

My pulse raced as I walked into the gym one night: only three weeks until the show opened as we added choreography to accompany the music. I climbed the bleachers and sat on the third row next to a couple of other sopranos. On the floor, Sue, the choreographer, showed a group of singers the dance steps for one of their numbers. When she'd finished, she walked over to a tall, dark-haired guy leaning against the wall. They turned to face the bleachers as they talked.

My, he looks familiar. I wondered. *Why's he pointing at me? Now I remember. He's the guy who pulled my hair at practice several months ago.*

Sue motioned for me to join them, saying, "Aaron got back yesterday from his military exercise and picked you as his dance partner." Little did I know, but his choice would change my life.

We had a lot of choreography to learn and memorize before the show. During practice Aaron held me in his arms while we gazed in each other's eyes and rehearsed the love songs. Then it happened. It stopped being a performance, and we fell in love.

Aaron drove me home from practice one night and parked the car overlooking the flight line where we could see the planes take off and land. In the dim moonlight we poured out our hearts and shared the dreams we each had for the future.

He said what I'd been craving, "Committed for life." He would love me and only me.

After a year of marriage why do I still feel insecure and have these awful nightmares about the abuse I suffered years before? *Where's my joy?*

While Aaron worked on Sundays I watched Christian programs on TV. One afternoon, I sat transfixed as I listened to several ladies talk about the abuse they'd lived through. Then they described the release from condemnation and fear they'd found through their faith in Jesus Christ.

I desperately wanted the forgiveness and joy they described!

When the televangelist asked the audience to bow their heads and pray, I joined them. Seated on the couch in our studio apartment, I gave my life to the Lord. I chose to believe God's love for me cleansed me from my past, covered my sins, and enabled me to start over again.

You may feel unworthy to approach God because of your sin or the sin someone dragged you through. Don't let an unsavory past stop you from giving your life to the Lord.

Prayer: God, I give my life to you. Heal the hurt and pain from my past. Give me a new life with You. Amen.

❧

Joyce Zook is the author of *12 Keys for Marriage Success* and is a speaker and Certified Professional Life Coach. Her business, Practical Christian Woman, encourages women to apply biblical principles in their everyday lives.

Lord, Send the Dolphins

Karissa Culbreath

We sat on the balcony of our cabin on our honeymoon cruise, basking in the glow of our recent vows. Hand-in-hand, we reminisced on the events of the past week. Our wedding day had started with a rainstorm and ended with a rainbow, and now we were on the last day of our honeymoon. It seemed as if there was nothing left to cap this perfect trip.

Then my husband said to me, "I wish we had seen some dolphins from our balcony. That would have made everything perfect."

I stood at the edge of the balcony and outstretched my arms and cried to the heavens, "Lord, send the dolphins!"

We both laughed hysterically as I looked out over the glistening water and watched the sun start its decent beyond the horizon. As waves crashed against the side of the ship, I noticed some movement in the water. "Look, Honey," I called, "there are fish down there."

My husband came to my side and looked down. "No, we are on the ninth deck. Those aren't fish; those are dolphins." An entire pod of dolphins had surfaced and were playfully swimming and jumping through the wake of our ship.

Was it possible? Had God heard me? Did God actually call down into the depths of the Atlantic Ocean and bid these beautiful animals to the surface?

Often we feel God doesn't hear us when we pray. The times when we are calling out to Him from the depths of our pain, frustration, and fear, we wonder, is anyone on the other end of the line? "Now this is the confidence that we have in Him, that if we ask anything according to His will, He hears us" (1 John 5:14, NKJV).

We have to be confident that we serve a God who hears our every prayer, even those prayers that never escape our lips, the prayers that we say in our hearts, the prayers that seem too audacious, too impossible even to utter. God operates at the level of the heart. Even if you can't imagine the words forming in your mouth, God still hears those requests.

And not only does He hear us, but "if we know that He hears us, whatever we ask, we know that we have the petitions that we have asked of Him" (1 John 5:15, NKJV). But it doesn't always seem He is responding, does it? He does respond; we just have to check our perspective.

From nine stories up, when I looked down at the water, I thought I was seeing something small, I thought I was seeing fish. I thought, *How nice, God responded to my request, not with the dolphins I had asked for, but fish are nice, too.*

Because of where I was standing above the water, the dolphins looked like fish. I almost ignored the "fish." Imagine if I had just brushed the sighting off! I would have missed the truth: God answered my prayer. I had settled for fish when God had given me dolphins.

This experience was just like every other time I had settled *for less* than God's very best for me. I settled for less because I felt unworthy. I settled for less because I was impatient. Even when I was willing to accept less, God gave me more than I could imagine.

What is it that you have been praying for? Take a look around you. Has God already answered that prayer in a way you didn't expect? Did you settle for less when God wanted to give you the best?

The words, "Lord, send the dolphins" became a rally cry in our marriage. For every obstacle that seems insurmountable, we look at each other and say, "Send the dolphins."

This was our reminder that not a prayer goes unheard or unanswered. If God called a whole pod of dolphins from the vast ocean, He could respond to any request we bring Him.

Prayer: God, we thank you for hearing our prayers. Help us to see your hand in our lives and never lose confidence that you hear us and answer every prayer.

❧

Karissa Culbreath, Ph.D. is a preacher, teacher, and professor. She has received awards for work in community engagement and activism. Her greatest passion and pride is her family: her husband Brian, and children, Mikaela and Ethan.

Without a Spot

Edna Ellison

I sat in church alone.

My husband was working that night, but I wanted to go to a church revival to see if God would show up. I needed a *Jesus overhaul*, as my husband had said often, when either of us was exhausted in body and spirit. After a few months at home with a newborn and a four-year old, my heart yearned for renewal. I took Jack to the preschool child care, and a moment later as I laid baby Patsy in a crib, I realized she had spit up on my dress. When I wiped the large milky spot off the front, I found the sleeve had split a seam. There it was: a large hole under my arm near the wet spot smelling of creamed rice cereal. A ragged corner of the seam was hanging out beneath the arm pit. I almost picked up my children to go home, but Jack was happily playing ball with other boys and Patsy was sleeping peacefully. Lifting my hands, I turned and tiptoed into our church sanctuary, where the service was beginning with a hymn.

Slipping into the back pew, I smiled. I had found a perfect spot for worshipping without anyone seeing me. I planned to sit alone, enjoy the singing, find the Holy Spirit to revive me through the corporate worship, and then leave without anyone noticing me, my ripped dress, or my unusual aroma.

The guest evangelist encouraged us with rousing words, but I was about to doze off, waiting for God to show up.

Startled, I heard the evangelist say, ". . . confess that Jesus is your Lord. Now."

No one moved. I scrunched down in my seat.

"Just stand up right where you are in this large sanctuary."

God showed up. "Edna, stand up and confess my name."

"Lord, I couldn't possibly stand up with this spit-up all over the front of my dress!"

"You need to show others you love me. Forget that spot. You wiped it clean."

No one moved. . . yet.

"If I stand and say anything, people will see this ragged hole under my arm."

"A tiny rip. You think anyone will notice *that*?"

Ten or eleven rows in front of me, an old lady stood. It was Mrs. Ellis, my fourth-grade school teacher. Humped over, leaning on the pew, she proclaimed loudly: "Jesus is my Lord!"

That did it. I had to move.

I stood erectly and confidently, not caring about the fragrant damp spot or the hole in my dress. "Jesus is my Lord!"

Suddenly people from all over the room stood up, shouting: "Jesus is my Lord!" "Jesus is MY Lord!" God showed up in many hiding hearts that night.

I celebrated with everyone: spotted, split-dress, and all!

O course, I knew God was with me in my home and in my heart every day, but something about worshiping with others touched my heart in a fresh way. Every one of us needs reminding of His Presence in our lives daily. No matter how many spots we have on us, God loves us, His precious children. Oh, how much He loves us! When we proclaim Him aloud, He must be beaming, as He rejoices over us with singing (Zeph. 3:17 NIV).

I praised God as he whispered a verse I knew: "For he chose us in him before the creation of the world. . . to be holy and blameless in his sight" (Eph. 1:4 NIV). I knew Jesus was the unblemished Lamb who accepted me with all my spit-up spots, rips, and smells.

Spend time today praising God for His great love for us, in spite of our holes and spots.

Prayer: O God, thank You for showing up in our lives every day. When we are down, You lift us up. When we are sad, You pour abundant joy into us. Thank You for loving us even when we have sinned. Forgive us for our sins and help us live a holy life even when we're holey. In Jesus' name, Amen.

Edna Ellison Ph.D.(www.ednaellison.com) accepted Jesus into her heart at age eleven. She's written over 400 Christian magazine articles and 31 books on mentoring/coaching and Christian living. With an earned Ph.D. in Language Arts, Dr. Ellison has spoken overseas in Frankfort, London, and Panama City. She is president of Advanced Writers and Speakers Association (AWSA) and the Beautiful Hat Society (www.thebeautifulhatsociety.com) for American mentors.

My BuddyPass

Lynne Leite

*W*hat *if all the stand-by seats are taken for the flights I need?* I worried. Getting a buddy pass ticket at a discount was a blessing, but not if I couldn't get a seat on the plane. *What if I get to Albuquerque and my anxiety flares up? What if? What if?*

Since the time I got the news I had won a scholarship to attend the CLASS Writers Conference in Albuquerque, I had been doing a pretty good job of remembering Jesus' words—"Don't worry about tomorrow, today has enough troubles of its own." But as the departure date approached, it was harder and harder to keep my anxiety at bay.

What if I get there and I have a panic attack? What if I'm alone when it happens? What if I have to take the train instead of a plane—how will I manage transferring trains at the Los Angeles Union Station? I tried to counter each "what if" with Jesus' reminder—"Don't worry about tomorrow, today has enough troubles of its own."

I knew those were true words, but I couldn't help but worry about my ability to attend the conference comfortably, to be in the moment, and to focus on all there was to learn. I had won a scholarship and that meant someone else might not be able to attend because of me. I felt an obligation to overcome my issues, once and for all, and go no matter what.

At the same time I also felt frustration rising up in me. "Lord," I cried out, "Why do I struggle with this? Why can't I be like normal people?"

I didn't get an answer, but I knew I needed to trust God to get me there. I truly believed He had given me this opportunity and He wanted me to go *as I was*, issues and all.

At that moment, a thought flashed through my mind, "Too bad Judee didn't get a scholarship. Then we could travel together and everything would be fine." Judee was a friend who had also applied for a scholarship to the conference; but I quickly dismissed the thought, knowing that at this late date, the chances she would get one were very slim.

Then later that day I got an email from Judee. "Lynne, I found out I am next on the list for a scholarship!" I was dumbfounded! Within hours of my conversation with the Lord there appeared to be a possible solution to my problem—one that would be a blessing in more ways than just having a traveling companion.

Still, I wondered: Was I really not ready to do this on my own? Was I still subject to the limitations of my anxiety? I so wanted to be that bold, fearless woman who would hop on a plane or train with confidence and relish every moment of every adventure. Instead I felt the Lord say to me, "Just come as you are. Come with your limitations. I want you here."

A second email came from Judee.

"I got the scholarship! I'm going to the conference! Do you still need a roommate and travel companion?" The plan was set. I felt a sense of peace wash over me and I let out a sigh of relief.

I now had a dear friend, a sister in Christ, to share this adventure with. I had someone to share my expenses and experiences, someone who shared my passion for stories and the Lord. We would take train trips, and brainstorm, and eat late night snacks, and so much more than if I had gone to the conference on my own.

God answered my prayer and exceeded my expectations—but not by taking away all my anxieties. I still struggle with traveling alone or being in crowds or venturing out to unfamiliar territories. I still hope that one day I will be completely free from any abnormal anxiety. But Jesus reminds me, "Don't worry about tomorrow. Think about today. And today I want you to come just as you are."

Prayer: Dear Lord, Thank you for loving me just as I am. Help me trust you with my issues, my todays, and all my tomorrows.

Lynne Leite is a writer, speaker, and storyteller. She is a contributor to the *Chicken Soup for the Soul* books and speaks at Christian women's events. You can learn more about Lynne online at www.CurlyGirl4God.com.

People of Hokkaido Island

Darlene Yahooskin Pena

It took many years through my childhood and young adult life to be able to arrive to the peace with my life conflicts and complications. Without the help of my red pony and the people of Hokkaido Island of Japan I might have not known how Jesus really loved me.

There was no one to help me learn about Jesus at home, but I could always go outside to the corral and see my red pony. As soon as I grabbed a handful of mane, I was on his back. My pain he felt, as he ran really fast letting the wind blow my tears away. My pony was red with a long mane and tail as the blue night. Like a whirlwind we were off to leave my enduring pain.

At night when I closed my eyes, my red pony and I rode in the night sky with his hooves leaping from star to star. The moon was shining on my beaded dress, while the mist of the air blew my buckskin dress fringe against my red pony's strong body. A smile on my face and content in my heart, I had a deep desire to move forward in life. As I go down memory lane today, thinking back into my youth, I know the pain was not necessary or needed.

I knew if I could be in the mountains with the smell of the tall pine trees, and the soothing sound of the running creek, I would be all right for this one night. My red pony took me to Cherry Creek and there at night I laid on his saddle blanket reaching for the stars. As I lay there I spread my fingers to see the stars through them as I was falling asleep with my red pony standing over me.

I was born a beautiful baby girl in 1954. In the photos of my mother and dad, they looked as if they loved me. Didn't anyone love me? I felt lonely, sad, and depressed. Many times my red pony and I would go for rides to help me escape a world of uncertainty.

I was always happy to see my Grandpa. He would let me help him roundup cattle, brand them, and go to summer cow camp with him. It was a place where I knew I would never be harmed or go hungry.

Then one day as a grown young woman, reading a *Western Horseman* magazine, an advertisement said, "Cowgirls needed for Montie Montana Wild West Show to go to Japan." I answered the ad. Sharing that I knew how to do the Lord's Prayer in the American Indian Language. My Indian dancing included the Butter Fly Dance and the Fancy Shawl Dance. To my excitement, the owner hired me! He said over the phone, "The Lord's Prayer will be the first performance you share with a Japanese audience."

I studied the country of Japan's culture, history, and the Inu Bear Clan Indians on the Island of Hokkaido. I would make two hundred dollars a week: a lot of money considering as a cowgirl I was only making fifteen dollars a day in America.

Our interpreter, Teddy, was a supervisor for a Japanese elementary school on the Island. He shared that he needed an American teacher.

Soon I was teaching fifth-grade students science and math. Thirty days later I wrote to my grandparents and mother to let them know I was working in Japan. I learned to write easy and light on the delicate rice paper.

Working for the Japanese school was teaching me my identity, defining my characteristics in strengths and weaknesses. My new Japanese friends who kindly took me in treated me with kindness and gentle words of friendship. Surely the Lord has funny ways of showing me how I am loved. In the reality of life, we do not always get the answers to our Why's. There among the people of Hokkaido Island, the Lord taught me that he'd never left me or had forsaken me. He was real in my heart!

Prayer: Lord, help us to invite you into our lives for deep peace and to fulfill the yearning in our hearts for You alone. Amen.

∽

It's been thirty years since **Darlene Yahooskin Pena** lived out those days in Japan with the Christian people on Hokkaido Island. She has never stopped thanking the Lord for sending her way the special red pony in her dreams and heart and then finding real peace through the Lord. Email: wahooapache@yahoo.com

Flash Drive Failure

Judee Stapp

O no! This can't be happening! In an instant my normal, routine day took a disastrous turn!

I sat down in my home office to work, slipped the little flash drive into my computer, and clicked to open it. The light on the front blinked on for a second and went out. I clicked a second, third, and then a fourth time . . . . nothing but a blink and then darkness! Why wasn't the flash drive opening so I could access the data? My whole life was on that flash drive! I took it out and looked at it carefully. The center part that fit into the USB port was loose, and a wire stuck out on the side! I taped around the entire apparatus and inserted it again. The light came on for a couple of seconds and then went out!

In retrospect I realized it had been crazy to put everything on that flash drive. I took it back and forth to work, always in too big of a rush to run backups.

Sometimes we take technology for granted, and I was scrambling to remember exactly what was on that small bit of metal and plastic—work logs, ideas, and fundraising projects. I had placed all my personal data on that drive including Christmas lists, family photos, and recipes. It held all my personal business documents, writing notes, and speeches. All lost! I felt angry and stupid! Why? Why had I put everything on that small, three-inch drive that wasn't even as big as my finger! It was just convenient to have my life always there in the pocket of my purse! But, now what?

I took the flash drive into three major computer stores to see if they could extract the data. The light would come on for a second or two and then go out just as it had for me. One clerk gave me a pamphlet for a data recovery company.

I rushed home to call, and the man who answered was confident. "Just mail it to us. We'll take the case apart, solder the wires, and recover your data."

I felt myself relax at that good news and asked, "About how much will that cost?"

"Oh," he replied, "between $1,000 and $2,700."

I felt my heart sink. There was no way I could afford that! Life went on, but I had to resort to re-creating documents, slowing down every project I worked on.

About a month later I was downloading flash drives of photos onto my computer. (Yes, I backed up on a regular basis now!) When I finished, I put the drives into the tray on my desk and noticed my useless flash drive there. I started to toss it into the trash to be rid of the daily reminder of my frustrating failure, but something made me pause.

Realizing that I hadn't asked God to help me, I knelt down with the flash drive in my hand and prayed. I told God that I knew I had been wrong to place my life in that piece of technology instead of in Him. I had put my trust in something I thought would always be there and it failed me as the things of this world will.

"Lord, from now on I will place my life in Your hands and never take any of my blessings for granted." I got up from my knees and plugged the flash drive into my computer with a hopeful heart. Wait! Was the light on the flash drive on? I couldn't believe it! Was it possible?

My hands were shaking as I opened the drive to view the files, and all of them seemed to be there! I quickly copied everything at once and pasted it on my computer. Once the download completed, the light on the flash drive went out, and nothing I could do would make it come on again! I quickly checked my hard drive to see what transferred.

Remarkably, everything was there! All the data was perfectly useable! Tears ran down my face. God had extended me grace and a real miracle! I framed that little flash drive, and I keep it on my desk as a reminder to place my trust in God and His power to restore, never give up hope, and always believe in miracles.

Prayer: Dear Lord, help me to remember "that we should not trust in ourselves, but in God who raises the dead" (2 Corinthians 1:9b NAS).

Judee Stapp is a speaker for Stonecroft Ministries who also speaks for women's events, retreats, and luncheons. She lives in Placentia, California with her husband, John. Contact her through her website: www.judeestapp.com

My Messy Life

Kathleen McQuain

My heart beat faster as the knot in my stomach grew. Frantically I looked around the room at the scattered toys, soiled burp cloths, and a carpet that desperately needed Stanley Steemer. Some of my friends were coming over to see my new baby, and I was too tired to tidy up for their visit. Nagged with a bad case of perfectionism, I worried about what they would think of me when they saw the chaos and disorder in my home. Consumed with my insecurities, I ignored my baby's cries. I yelled at my four-year-old to pick up his toys. The doorbell rang.

My friends swooped in with scrumptious food, baby gifts, and even a special treat for big brother. No one seemed to notice the clutter that bothered me so much. Momentarily, I set aside my fears and allowed my friends to love on me and my kids. After they left, I marveled at their love and acceptance. I remembered lots of smiles and hugs and lighthearted conversation. It slowly dawned on me that they really wanted me and my friendship, whether my house was clean or not!

Sometimes the untidy details of my life or my personal flaws keep me from approaching God or opening the door of my heart to him. I remember a time, shortly after the death of my mother, when I fell into a dark pit of depression. In my grief, I began pushing everyone away, including God. My husband bore the brunt of my misery. With each passing day, my angry outbursts and moodiness diminished the look of love in his eyes. One day, I curled up under the covers on my bed trying to disappear, doubtful I could ever be happy again. I had quite a pity party, convinced that nobody loved me, not even God.

But God refused to leave me in my pit of despair, and He certainly didn't wait for me to clean up my act. Instead He joined me in my joyless cocoon, suffusing it with light and bathing me with His amazing love. I remember sitting on the edge looking down into the darkness, stunned that I had managed to climb out. Then God overwhelmed me with the sweetness of His presence, and the realization that He had pulled me out of the darkness. Indeed, He had kept his promise to never leave me nor forsake me (See Hebrews 13:4.). I pulled the covers away from my face and saw my husband sitting by the side of our bed, waiting patiently for my return. In his eyes, I found the love and acceptance I so desperately craved.

The Bible offers numerous examples of desperate people with disorderly lives who, like me, searched for love and acceptance. For instance, a Samaritan woman surprisingly found more than water at the town well. (See John 4.) Jesus initiated a conversation with her and exposed the sordid details of her life, but he also offered her the gift of living water. She, in turn, rushed to tell her neighbors the good news that the Messiah had come. Truly, God doesn't wait for perfect people to hunt him down. He seeks out the poor and the sick and the saints and the sinners. He uncovers our woundedness and makes something beautiful out of the ugliness of our lives.

The Psalmist describes it this way: "I waited patiently for the LORD; he inclined to me and heard my cry. He drew me up from the pit of destruction, out of the miry bog, and set my feet upon a rock, making my steps secure. He put a new song in my mouth, a song of praise to our God. Many will see and fear, and put their trust in the LORD . . ." (Psalm 40:1-3 ESV).

My life and I remain a bit messy. In fact, it's finally sunk in that I just won't have perfection this side of heaven! So I'm learning to relax more and stress less. Each day I must choose to believe that God loves me no matter what, and just like the psalmist, that makes me want to sing for joy.

Prayer: Dear Lord, help me to keep singing your song so that others will hear and put their trust in you. Amen.

∾

Kathleen McQuain is a writer, speaker, and Bible study teacher who lives in Phoenix, Arizona, with her husband Danny. Contact her at www.thisdayministry.com.

Pink Cast and a Walker

Barbara Amy

Wellness Week is my time of year. Sponsored by First Place 4 Health and held in Round Top, Texas, the week is full of opportunities to exercise, eat healthy, listen to inspirational speakers, and look at what His Word has to say. I am the sound technician and usually bring all the audio visual equipment.

Three weeks before the event one year, I had foot surgery, so I was sporting a pink cast and scooting around on an all-terrain knee walker.

Excuses ran through my mind. This was a "wellness week" which meant that there would be different forms of exercise—which I could not participate in. Besides, I didn't want to be a burden to anyone. I had other good excuses and some were probably legitimate.

I called a friend, asking her to pray for me about loading the equipment and luggage I needed to take with me. When I hung up the phone, I received a text from another friend asking if she could follow me to the retreat center. I knew God was answering the prayer for help. My friend spent the night with me, helped me load my car and unload it at the retreat center. She even helped me to set up all the technical equipment.

On our schedule there was a listing for something called "The Half"—half of a 5K or 1.6 miles. I could not do it because I was in a pink cast scooting around on a knee walker. I threw myself a grand pity party in my room, whining to God about this pink cast and knee walker. I got the distinct impression on my heart, "Scoot the race on your walker for Me and I will give you the strength you need to finish the race." The race was not about finishing first but whether I would be obedient to what He was asking of me. I was tempted on several occasions during the race to stop, but then someone always came to encourage me to press on. With each step, I kept repeating Philippians 4:13, "I can do all things through Christ who strengthens me."

It would have been easy to sit during the race and use the excuses I had in my mind. If I had done that, I never would have experienced His love and strength—plus I may not have gotten the award for the "Biggest Loser," losing 12 pounds in just 6 days.

So scoot toward God no matter what challenge you may have. He is waiting at the finish line with arms open wide.

Prayer: Father, help us lay down our excuses and come to you, even if it is with a pink cast and an all-terrain walker. Amen.

Barbara Amy lives in Beaumont, Texas, with her black-mouth cur, Hercules. One of her passions is to help churches with Vacation Bible Schools across the country during the summer. At the present time she has lost 35 pounds towards a goal of 100 using the First Place 4 Health program.

Do You Believe?

Vicki Kessler

Do you believe in miracles? I'm not sure I always did until I watched one unfold. It has been almost five years since I received the first call.

My sister called to say her husband Danny, my brother in law, had leukemia—a rare aggressive type. I was stunned. And then she said chemo would start on Monday.

I flew to Denver. The prognosis was grim. Danny might not make it. After a week in intensive care he pulled through, received a transplant, and recovered. Everyone was ecstatic. Not that it was easy, but he made it.

Then on a cold day in October I got another dreaded call. Danny was headed to the hospital. His system was toxic. My sister's voice was strained.

By the time I got to Denver, my sister was spent—emotionally and physically. I gave her a hug and all she said was "it's your turn." I walked into the room noticing the room location, private nurse, the 24 IVs, ventilator, and other machines. Each one indicated the seriousness of the situation. She rested and I monitored the screens and the people. Every hour, I texted the family an update. I prayed over Danny, thanking God for the time with Danny, asking for comfort, strength, and for the angels to guide him home to Jesus. Mid prayer I thought, *I am praying the wrong prayer*. So I started praying for healing and strength. A peace came over me and I remembered Philippians 4:13: "I can do all things through Christ who strengthens me" (NKJV).

Each hour that passed came with a triumph. One machine/IV at a time was removed. By early morning the doctors were baffled, wondering how it happened. But I knew. Reminded of Hebrews 11:1, "Now faith is being sure of what we hope for and certain of what we do not see" (NIV). Danny surprised everyone. By mid-morning Danny was up and laughing. Later we talked about it. He had heard me praying over him. He thought I was an angel. I told him I felt God saying it wasn't his time yet. There was more for him to accomplish. Psalm 77:4 says, "you are the God who performs miracles."

I once thought miracles only occurred in Bible times. Not anymore. I invite you to consider, do you believe in miracles?

Prayer: Dear Lord, thank you for continued miracles. Help me be alert to Your miracles that occur around me. Amen.

❧

Vicki Kessler is the mother of three. She enjoys cooking, quilting, spending time with her three grandchildren, and serving in the women's ministry at her church.

The Journey

Glorianna Yee

I crawled up from a dark and shady fissure
To discover it's a scary dangerous thing.
I must admit the truth of human nature
And forfeit my throne to God the mighty King.
To live in darkness is a dreadful life
While coming into th' light is just as wrong.
I'm drowning in the darkness full of strife
And running from the Light and His love song.
Why can't I understand that He loves me?
Accepting me, yes me, for who I am,
Despite the broken helplessness in me,
Because I'll always be His needy lamb.
In darkness I was lost, but th' light has found.
I once was chained but now I am unbound.

Each of us on the Christian journey can keep on walking because there is hope. Glorianna Yee wrote this poem as her composition for this book of articles. Her advisers think it is a valued addition to the book, to show our diversity as Christians depending on Christ daily.

Prayer: Dear Lord, help me run to you even in the darkness. Amen.

❧

Glorianna Yee is a writer who lives in the foothills of

Albuquerque, New Mexico. She loves the sunlight but dislikes reading poetry and offers the sonnet published in this book. May you find it a blessing for your soul.

Let the Little Children Come

Tanzia Prosper

When a young child publicly proclaims belief in the Lord Jesus Christ, well-meaning adults sometimes challenge whether the decision is authentic. As the child grows into adulthood, these seeds of skepticism grow and the now-adult child gets tangled in cycles of doubt. Unsure of their salvation, these children come to Jesus over and over again believing that their childhood decision for Christ was not enough.

Not long ago, at a youth discipleship event, I met young ladies who made decisions for Christ. Five or six of those teary-eyed females were there to receive Christ—again. After hearing the speaker challenge the sincerity of a childhood belief, they weren't sure if their childhood conversions had been genuine. Perhaps skeptics plant doubt in an effort to bring about what they believe will be more authentic conversion experiences, but what kind of damage might be caused in a life that learns not to trust the surety of their salvation? How long will they struggle with uncertainty about their faith in God? We should be careful not to plant seeds of doubt.

Several years ago a friend shared that her young children expressed a desire to receive Christ as their Savior, but her husband had not allowed it, because he questioned the validity of childhood belief. He believed that a person needs a full understanding of redemption before confessing belief and that a child cannot make a genuine decision for Christ. However, even an adult can't possibly understand everything about redemption. Who can comprehend the love of God? Belief in Christ is not a function of age, but a decision, through the work of the Spirit, that even a child can make. (See Mark 10:14.) God is faithful and when we believe, He begins to teach us all we need to know. This learning and growing is a lifetime process. Simple belief is where God meets us all. (See Matthew 18:3.)

As a seven-year old, I proclaimed, "I want to be a follower of Jesus." What had compelled me, at this early age, to arrive at such a decision? The Holy Spirit used two ideas to draw me to consider Jesus as a young child. The first was eternity and the second was hell. Trying to understand the concept of forever was overwhelming. The thought of spending forever in hell was even more disturbing. Jesus could save me from this outcome, and that was all I needed to know.

My baptism was exciting. A mirror hung over the pool, allowing the congregation to watch. My grandmother began to sing an acappella chorus of "Let us go down to Jordan, religion is so sweet." My grandfather held me afloat on my right side, and the preacher stood on my left as he repeated, in his booming baritone voice, my profession of faith. I remembered being impressed that he remembered my exact words. Unnoticed by either of them, a small spider swam towards me trying to find a way out. In my imagination it was going to make its way up my baptism gown, and crawl onto me. But I knew enough not to interrupt the baptism event. After they submerged me under the water, my cousins, who were all crouched down around the baptism pool, informed me that I came up with a scream.

I didn't recall the scream, but I couldn't deny it. I figured that either my fear of the spider got the best of me, or the demons screamed on the way out. God honored my request to be a follower of Jesus, and His work continues in my life today.

God brought me to a better understanding of my sinful condition and redemption at age twenty-one when a good friend invited me to Bible study.

Where would I have been without that childhood decision? We are instructed to believe on the Lord Jesus Christ; the result is that we will be saved. (See Acts 16:31.) We don't need to over complicate it. Avoid being the seed of doubt and skepticism in the heart that has believed as a child. Biblical childhood decisions for Christ are genuine, and it is not our assigned mission to cast doubt on them. Let the children come.

Children don't know everything about belief when they make a decision for Christ, but who does? It is God's wisdom that we are dependent upon to save us, not our own.

Prayer: Dear Father, please give me confidence in my decision to accept your gift of salvation through Jesus Christ, and help me to celebrate your work of belief in both the old and young. Keep me from being the seed of doubt in the heart that has believed, in Jesus' name. Amen.

Tanzia Prosper is a native of New Orleans, Louisiana, but has called New Mexico home for the past nine years. She is passionate about carrying the message of Christ into the world, especially through writing.

Imperfection Is Not Failure

Victoria Johnston

For I know the plans I have for you," declares the Lord, "plans to prosper you and not to harm you, plans to give you hope and a future (Jeremiah 29:11 NIV).

I was born and raised in East Texas. My father was a drinker who had nothing to do with me. He and my mother divorced when I was two. He said he would see me when I was 18. We never heard from him again. This abandonment started my life journey longing to be loved and accepted by a father I never knew. My mom was a loving mom now raising me alone—or so I thought.

While working she met a big bear of a man. He was protective of my mother. They were soon married, but afterward something changed. He became overly jealous and controlling. This attitude soon turned into physical abuse of my mom and emotional abuse for my brother and me. But even then I longed for my stepdad to spend time with me. We walked on eggshells at home. I never felt I fit at home or anywhere else. I did think, however, if I could behave I could bring peace to my home. I equated acceptance with love and peace.

Peace was elusive and inconsistent. I longed for it. I would do whatever I had to do to make it happen. But I could not make the peace stay or my stepdad love me. I eventually started suffering from depression. I had an uncontrollable fear that I could not shake or overcome, and I stopped eating and sleeping.

Then at school I saw a man who came for lunch with some of the students. I learned he was the pastor at the local church. He was a young man, with a beautiful wife and two sons, but he looked more like a hippie than a pastor. As my depression became worse, my mom contacted him and asked if he would talk with me. He agreed. He came and we talked. I honestly do not remember the conversation part. I do remember the time he told me about Jesus: He told me Jesus was God in the flesh. He said *Jesus loved me* for who I was. I did not have to work for His love or acceptance. He told me Jesus was God's Son and He came to earth and lived a sinless life. He died on the cross for my disobedience to His law. He said not only did Jesus die for me, but also He came back to life just for me. And He wanted to spend time with me! Wow, I could hardly believe it. He told me that if I believed Jesus was God and He died on the cross for my sins and rose again from the dead, I could ask Him to come and enter my heart and He would be Lord and Savior of my life. I could finally have a relationship with my Father. The relationship I longed for.

I prayed and asked Jesus into my heart that day. And there it was: the peace that I longed for. In Philippians 4:7 God calls this "the peace that passes all understanding" (KJV). It was amazing. The fear was gone, and I was finally accepted and finally home. I slept for the first time in a long time. I began reading His Word and learning more about Him. I was able to talk to Him in prayer. I read in John 14:27 "My peace I give to you; not as the world gives do I give to you. Do not let your heart be trouble nor let it be fearful." I loved my time with Him.

I did not know how accepting Christ would change my life, and in the future I would meet an amazing Christian man, Bobby Johnston, who would become my husband. Bobby was raised in a Christian home. I learned from him and his dad about dads on earth who do love us and want to spend time with us and accept us for who we are. They are not perfect, but imperfection is OK. I have a Heavenly Father who is. He has always been there. I do not have to worry that I am alone. His love is sufficient, and God's peace is eternal. I know God loves me for who I am and His love is enough for me.

God loves us for who we are and He will never leave us. We can hide in His loving, accepting arms and finally find rest.

Prayer: Dear Lord, Thank you for loving me as I am. I love you and I am so thankful for You and Your Word that assures me each day that You care for me. Amen.

❧

Victoria Johnston is a singer, writer, speaker, and certified personality trainer. She lives in Albuquerque with her husband of 20 years. She loves crafts and hopes to start quilting soon.

Lessons from Tractors and Cattle

David Allen

When I was five years old, I had two unusual experiences on my grandparents' farm near Hemet, California. The first one happened as soon as Dad brought me up from our San Diego home for a visit. There was Grandpa Allen alone in the field laying irrigation pipes. The pipes were on a flat bed wagon pulled by a slow-moving tractor. Grandpa went back and forth laying a few pipes, and then straightening out the steering wheel to keep the tractor on course.

When I arrived, he picked me up, set me in the driver's seat, and showed me how to throttle and steer the machine. Not yet having the inhibitions of later life, I didn't know this was something I wasn't supposed to be able to do. So this five-year-old learned how to drive a farm tractor—and made work easier for someone else.

The second experience also took place on my grandparents' farm. My father inherited their dairy farm in San Diego, and he often sent the calves to Grandpa from about the time they were six months old until they were ready to give birth to their first calf. This well-irrigated, one-hundred acre spread had plenty of fresh grass and was kind of a bovine heaven on earth.

One time I went for a walk, and soon I was playing on a dirt road. Oblivious to the outside world, I continued playing—until I heard my grandmother calling, "Oh David Boy! It's time for lunch."

When I stood up, I saw something that terrified me. I was surrounded by twenty or more curious yearling cattle. My fear was justified. In every way the cattle were physically superior to me and could have caused serious bodily harm—or even death if they stampeded. I sat paralyzed in fright, and soon my grandmother called again, "O David Boy, why haven't you come to lunch?"

Crying, I said, "I can't Grandma. These cows are standing all around me!"

"O! Just pick up a stick or stone," she said, "and throw it at them."

I really didn't believe her, but seeing no other alternative, I did as she said. To my total amazement, they scattered. I spent the next few minutes throwing anything I found and yelling, "Go away, you big mean old cows." Then, triumphantly I came home to lunch.

Have you ever faced a daunting task or challenge? What would you be able to do if you weren't held back by adult inhibitions like doubt and fear? A wise person once said, "Face the fear, and do it anyway." That was great advice for a five-year-old boy—or for anyone at any age. The philosopher Mencius said, "The truly great person never fully ceases to have the heart of a child."

Isaiah 40:31 says, ". . . but those who hope in the Lord will renew their strength" (NIV). You will be amazed by your potential if you will only step out of your comfort zone and attempt great things.

Prayer: Lord, help me rediscover the dreams and confidence of my youth. Help me to be an inspiration and example to others. May we expect great things from You and attempt great things for You. Amen.

∽

David Allen taught for more than eight years in the jail system. Now an award-winning speaker, his most requested topic include the four personalities and his view from the jail.

Message from a Butterfly

Marilyn Neuber Larson

D on't wait up for me," my husband said on his way out one Saturday morning. "I'm working late."

Our marriage was in crisis and fear clutched my stomach. I knew I had to keep going, so I grabbed lawn tools. The backyard had grown as out-of-control as our relationship.

Although I grew up in church, my prayers were different that day. "Dear Jesus, I'm terrified. Is our marriage over? How can I survive alone? Show me what to do." I pulled weeds and continued my petitions. "Lord, forgive me. I'm sorry for my part in our troubled marriage." All day I poured out my troubles and talked to Jesus. How comforting to know he listened and cared.

In late afternoon, I stuffed scraggly branches into a bag. "Lord, give me a sign." I started toward the trash can, but stopped and held my breath. A magnificent Monarch butterfly fluttered into my world and rested on a faded lavender flower.

"This can't be," I told myself. "It's almost November."

Sunlight glistened on orange and black wings—a gift from God. The tiny creature stepped across a leaf and pressed its wings together like hands folded in prayer.

A Bible verse floated into my mind from childhood. "Trust in the Lord with all your heart, and lean not on your own understanding; in all your ways acknowledge Him, and He shall direct your paths" (Proverbs 3:5-6 NKJV).

It was as if Jesus whispered, "Trust me, Marilyn. I just want you to trust me." As a child I had invited Jesus into my heart, yet that day in the yard, we entered into an awesome relationship. How exciting to call to him in prayer, and he spoke to me whenever I opened the Bible. Sometimes when I asked a question, words jumped off the page, and I knew he answered.

Butterflies became a symbol as my husband and I worked to hold our marriage together. For a while it seemed possible to overcome our problems, but it was not to be.

When fear threatened, I felt as weak as a caterpillar, yet my relationship with Jesus strengthened as he directed my steps through the painful metamorphosis of divorce.

Little did I dream I'd emerge from my cocoon stronger, happier, and ready to fly. Often when the path became rocky, a fragile butterfly fluttered into my world, reminding me to trust.

The day our divorce was to be final, I drove into the dismal catacombs of underground parking. Red taillights winked as a car backed out, leaving a whiff of exhaust fumes while I parked. My feet felt heavy when I climbed the stairs to the street.

"Jesus," I prayed, "I'm still not sure about this divorce. Is this my path? Could you give me a sign?"

On the sidewalk brilliant sunshine reflected that concrete world. I squinted and glanced down, but when a shadow crossed my path, I looked up. A gorgeous yellow-and-black Tiger Swallowtail butterfly danced just above my head. Sunlight filtered through its translucent wings like stained glass.

"This is my sign," I exclaimed.

The magnificent creature circled my head twice, as if to say, "Now watch me, Marilyn." It flew parallel to the courthouse as if it followed a distinct path. When it reached the edge of the building the butterfly turned the corner and disappeared. It was as if the path for my life had turned a corner.

The message rang in my ears, "Trust me, Marilyn. In the next few minutes you will turn the corner, but I will be with you. I will never leave you or forsake you."

My heart pounded, and my knees trembled, but I was not afraid, for Jesus walked with me to my new life. The path led up the courthouse steps, and I emerged from my divorce cocoon ready to fly.

On that October day butterflies became my sign, and I'm delighted to share them with you. Remember, whenever a butterfly flutters into your world, Jesus whispers, "Trust me, I just want you to trust me."

Prayer: Dear Jesus, thank you for your loving relationship and thanks for sending such a unique reminder of your awesome presence. Amen.

∽

Marilyn Neuber Larson is a writer and speaker in Albuquerque, New Mexico. After being single for years, God had a surprise. She retired from teaching school to become Pumpkin Queen when she married Bill, her farmer hero.

Through Suffering There's...Hope?

Symphony Bassett

The pain . . . the blood.

I had caught myself carving words into my arm. *What was I doing? I have been having suicidal thoughts for eight years now.* I was fine. At least that's what I led everyone to believe. Have I really been keeping my emotions hidden for so long that I now feel its necessity to cause physical harm? All this to prove to myself that I'm still alive and still have feelings. Is all this trouble worth the consequences?

I'm not sure. All I know is I need help!

If I'm really willing to hurt myself, then who is to say it won't be worse in two years? I've been told by many people (especially my step-father) that I'm worthless and I'll never get anywhere in life. *Is that really true? Do I have a future?* Those thoughts caused this problem in the first place.

Now that I have told you what has been going through my head, let me take you back a few years—sixteen to be exact. My mother; beautiful, strong-willed, and pregnant. My father; drunk, lousy, and abusive. They had a girl: me. They said it was a wonderful day full of laughter and love.

I have grown up (so far) living with my mother. She is kind and sweet, helping when she can—trying to make everyone happy. My father was never around. He died when I was eleven.

When I was seven, my mom remarried. The man's name was Zane. He seemed nice for the first year or so. They were happy. They had two kids together. Lovely kids, but definitely difficult to deal with. It was hard to get used to (I mean, you would have trouble too if you had three strangers suddenly dropped into your perfect life!) I didn't know what to do, so I shut everyone out.

Zane never took care of the kids when he was home. When my mom was home, she was always busy cleaning, so I took care of the kids. When Zane was mad at me, he would discipline me. Most of the time he would lose his temper, leaving welts and bruises. I never told my mom, because I didn't think she would believe me.

Ten years of playing the parent was hard to do, but I survived—mostly.

I was so scared and overwhelmed that I started having suicidal thoughts. I tried every way I could think of to end my life, but something or someone always interrupted me. Instead of trying to end my life, I jumped from one guy to another, hoping to find love, affection, and someone who was willing to care and protect me. But every guy I've run to has used and abused my trust and affection. I have lost hope.

I'm afraid of men and teenaged boys, because Zane threatened to kill me many times. Many teenaged boys have tried to abuse me sexually.

You could say I'm lucky. I got away before they could do anything, but they still scare me. I hide the fear, so no one knows what's going on. I don't want to worry my mom or get confronted. I no longer know where to go, what to do, or whom to trust. But I do know that God has a plan for my future. I'm going to trust Him to lead me in the way He wants me to go.

Prayer: Lord, help me, I don't know where to go from here. I'm confused and lost. Even though sometimes I don't feel as if You're real, I know You've been the One keeping me here. Amen.

∽

Symphony Bassett is sixteen years old. She feels she now has a wonderful family. She loves art and hopes to major in photography in college. Writing has become her second hobby.

He Has Broken Every Chain

Sativa Martinez-Olmstead

As I sat in the emergency room, a nurse inspected the cuts, scars, and burns on my wrists. Other doctors ran a drug test on me. I looked down at my feet that dangled off the hospital chair and suicidal thoughts began to run through my mind. Little did I know, this would be the first day of the next year spent in mental hospitals and rehab.

What made me end up in places like this? I thought.

Growing up, I never knew what happiness felt like. I was abused as a little girl. When I was five, my biological mom left me. I moved in with my dad and stepmom. I felt I was unloved so I started cutting myself in fifth grade. Living in my home was difficult because of domestic violence and drugs. I remember some nights I stayed up watching the police invade my home. I hated the sound of their feet walking on all the broken glass I knew I would have to clean up later. I built up a hatred toward police officers because of all the times they took my dad.

At age fourteen, I was asked to write a witness statement against my father to keep him in prison. That day I knew this kind of life was not normal. I had no mom. No love from my parents. I was depressed, and I suffered from insomnia. I no longer cared about myself or anyone else. I saw no purpose for my life. After many years, I decided I was done—I didn't want to live life anymore.

I opened the medicine cabinet, reached for a bottle of pills, swallowed all of them and hoped to die. I woke up and found myself vomiting in my bathroom. No one else knew. After this, I continued cutting. Eventually, I started burning myself because I was entangled in all the mental, physical, and emotional chains that Satan had me in.

When I entered high school, I was introduced to drugs. I started with marijuana and ended up on meth. I thought I needed to be high just to get through each day. I let drugs take hold of my life and control me. I was a prisoner in Satan's cell, and thought I could never be free. All I ever wanted was to be loved. I started chatting online with random men. I thought all the attention they were giving me was love. But I was wrong.

I was a master at hiding my feelings and living a double life, but when the truth was finally revealed, I was sent to the emergency room because my parents feared for my life. From there I went to mental hospitals and rehab. Doctors filled me with medication and told me I was "sick." Everything was taken away from me: my clothes, my shoelaces, my education, my freedom, and my dignity. These hospitals made me believe that I was not a human being, but a robot.

It wasn't until I came to a place called Teen Challenge of New Mexico that I finally was freed from all these chains. As soon as I walked through the doors of Teen Challenge, I could feel an overwhelming sense of peace. I saw the love the other girls had and I knew I wanted it. One night we were having a revival, and I remember being on my knees praying. Jesus Christ came into my heart and I could feel the chains falling and love entering into my heart for the first time. Even though I felt unworthy, I began to understand what love really is. By God's grace I have been delivered from depression, insomnia, drug addiction, and all the lies I believed in. Jesus Christ holds the keys that free us from the chains of the enemy. All we have to do is believe.

Prayer: Dear God, thank you that you love each of us so much that you sent your only Son to die for the punishment of our sins. I thank you and praise you, Lord Jesus, for holding the keys that set us free from chains and bondage. Amen.

∼

Sativa Martinez-Olmstead was born and raised in Albuquerque, New Mexico, and is seventeen and enjoying her last year of high school. After Teen Challenge, Sativa hopes to go to art college and become a photographer.

From Ashes to Beauty!

Mariah Baca-Chavez

L ong before I was ever born, God was at work forming and shaping the purposes of my life. God created my inmost being and knit me together in my mother's womb. (See Psalm 139.) I was born addicted to heroin and meth. Though I had to go through a period of detoxification, God had a plan for my life. The enemy tried to destroy what God meant for good. Before I was four years old, I was sexually abused two times; one by my step-dad and one by his nephew. As I got older, the hurt in my heart intensified. It was difficult for me to forgive my step-dad, because I felt he had taken away some of my dignity.

I was taken away from my mom at age five, because of the drugs and the wrong choices she was making. My real father was never involved in my life. But when I was five, my grandmother adopted me. Then he visited me every holiday and on my birthdays to bring me gifts and talk to me. At age eight my father died from an overdose. My mom also visited my siblings and me, but she always made promises she could never keep. Though my mother and father deserted me, my Father in heaven never left my side.

My grandmother exemplified this new godly meaning to my life. She took my siblings and me to become a part of a close knit body of believers. My grandmother did her best to serve the church and community. She began to experience sickness in the winter of 2010. My education suffered because of my growing responsibility to take care of my grandmother. My small glimpse of happiness quickly turned to a nightmare when she passed away from cancer.

When I was ten years old, God had planned everything out. Years before, my grandmother had asked a family at church to adopt my brother, sister, and me if anything happened to her. I went to a godly family that cared, loved, protected, and brought up my siblings and me. In the beginning I loved my family, but I never knew what a normal family was like. Now I had a mom, dad, and four siblings. I did not have to worry about being the mother role model or making decisions kids my age should not be making. Even though I was an intelligent, kind, peaceful, servant girl who loved God, I began to develop wrong choices. I would lie because I had fear. I became depressed. I built up walls towards my parents and I had no idea how to build a relationship with them. I lived a secret life. My parents tried everything they could to help me. I went from counselors to a psychiatrist, but it seemed nothing was working. I knew I needed more help from somewhere, because I was only hurting myself and my family. Then, my mom found Teen Challenge!

At Teen Challenge I have learned to do everything unto the Lord and not for myself or others. He took my ashes and made them beauty. I have obtained more conviction and I learned to appreciate the things I have. I am God's masterpiece, and He is at work in my life. Isaiah 64:8 says, "Yet, O Lord, you are our Father. We are the clay, you are the potter; we are all the work of your hand" (NIV).

Prayer: Dear Lord, thank you for changing me. You've taken the ashes of my life and made me new. Amen.

∽

Mariah Baca-Chavez is sixteen and desires to become a pediatric oncologist. She wants to continue serving the Lord for the rest of her life. She loves to run, play the guitar, and tell others about God.

His Cup of Grace

Madison Schneider

For he chose us in him before the creation of the world to be holy and blameless in his sight. In love he predestined us to be adopted as his sons through Jesus Christ, in accordance with his pleasure and will (Ephesians 1:4-5 NIV).

Crunch, crunch! Charmay's mom cleaned up the broken glass from the dining room's tiled floor.

"Mommy what happened?" Charmay asked.

"Don't come over here without your shoes!"

"Why do people throw rocks through our window when they can knock on the door?" the five-year-old asked.

"They're bad people, Baby… where's Isaiah?"

"He's in his room, Mommy."

Sigh. "Why do I always get us into theses messes?"

Charmay and Isaiah grew up faster than most kids. Their dad was in prison. Their mom was involved in drugs, which often impaired her thinking. Isaiah and Charmay were left home alone many nights. No one tucked them in. No one made sure they were safe.

Charmay remembered one night when her mom was gone and her mom's best friend showed up in the middle of the night. Normally, this woman cared for them when their mom was gone, but this night was different. She demanded to know where Charmay's mom was. When Charmay said, "She's not here," the woman, along with her dad and her brother, barged in and looted the house. Charmay was five, and her brother was six when this happened. They didn't understand what went on. How could they? Robbery was normal in their lives.

The next morning their mom came home and was furious, but not at being robbed. She was mad at them. She began to curse them and beat them uncontrollably. Their mom and her best friend had just gotten into a fight and the kids were oblivious because they were accustomed to volcanic disputations.

Isaiah and Charmay went to school like ordinary kids. They didn't realize their situation was unusual until a representative from Child Protective Service questioned them. That day the state intervened and removed the siblings from their home. Foster care became their new home. Isaiah and Charmay beat up other kids to numb their pain and stuff their hurt. When people tried to converse with them, the conversation was like talking to cold, lifeless beings. Before long, a family adopted them. The family went through the tedious classes, hearings, and paper work to be able to finally call the children their own.

Isaiah was eight and Charmay was seven when the adoption occurred. Their new life seemed luxurious; they had food, clothes, a stable income, and a family. Their new family loved them so much, but Isaiah and Charmay refuted their love. They were driven by hate, lies, and manipulation. At times they wanted to let go and experience true joy, yet they feared the release of all they'd ever known. The two of them working together made everyone miserable.

As Charmay became a teenager, she wanted to experience independence. Even though her parents taught her about the Lord, she couldn't understand why He would love her unconditionally. She began looking for answers and love in different places. She involved herself in the darkness of witchcraft and the perversion of pornography. As she became darker and empty, her parents did their best to love her and guide her. It's difficult to love someone who pushes people away. Her parents understood that she was deceived and entertained darkness.

Charmay wanted to escape her past and her problems, so she planned to run away with a man she'd met online. She told one of her sisters about the plan and the sister told her parents. Charmay's plans were intercepted. Years of undeleted hurt piled up, which became so overwhelming even Charmay couldn't handle it.

Her parents sent her to Teen Challenge, where she realized the Lord adopted her into His family. God was always there. When the Lord reached out to her, she grabbed His hand and never let go. The Lord transformed Charmay. She not only has five brothers and two sisters, but she's enthralled to have dozens of Christian brothers and sisters.

When Charmay was adopted by her family, she changed her name to Madison. Today, by God's grace, she's not defined by her past.

Prayer: Dear Heavenly Father, thank you for always accepting me every time I fall. Allow me to be the light you have created me to be. Amen.

❧

Madison Schneider is a young American patriot who has a heart for our military and a passion to write. She wants to be a preacher to share her experiences with others. She says, "This is my story." May she always find peace in Christ and become more godly each day of her future.

Worst Dad in the World

Jesse Florea

Some dads cherish their "World's Greatest Father" coffee mugs. Other fathers hold a tender place in their hearts for a sawn-off piece of two-by-four with a photo of their child glued to it that reads, "Chip off the old block." But I've grown to treasure my daughter's special name for me: "Worst Dad in the World."

I didn't always appreciate this title. The daddy/daughter bond is a special one. We always had nicknames for each other. She liked to call me "paj" (short for *padre*). And no matter how old she got, I always saw her as "Daddy's Little Girl."

I earned my unflattering moniker in the Colorado outdoors. Wanting quality family time, I pushed my daughter to do things outside her comfort zone. Sometimes it was twenty-mile bike rides. Other times it was hikes up one of Colorado's 14,000-foot mountains. She went with me on these adventures, and then I'd wonder if I was building memories or resentment.

Check out this actual conversation from a hike up Mount Democrat in Breckenridge, Colorado, where I first earned my title.

Daughter: I want to go back to the car.

Me: But we're over halfway to the top.

Daughter: I can't go any farther.

Me: Just make it to that switchback up there and you can have some beef jerky.

Daughter: How about if I just make it to that big rock?

Me: No, you can get to that switchback.

Daughter: You're the worst dad in the world!

Echo off mountain: World, world, world, world.

At first I thought a lack of oxygen had blurred my daughter's ability to reason and caused her to call me the world's worst dad. But the symptoms of altitude sickness include headache, nausea, dizziness and sleepiness. Shouting unflattering names doesn't appear to be caused by a lack of oxygen, although my daughter did complain of a headache.

My headache could be found walking right next to me—just kidding— as we neared the top of the mountain.

And we did make it to the top. It took nearly three hours and two miles of hiking to reach 14,152 feet above sea level. Standing at the summit, we were treated to majestic views in 360 degrees. The sense of accomplishment was overwhelming.

Me: Sweetie, you're standing at an elevation and seeing a landscape that only a fraction of the world's population will ever experience.

Daughter: Can I have some more beef jerky?

Yet I couldn't help but think by making it to the summit that my daughter had learned something about perseverance, relying on God's strength, working as a team, and encouraging each other.

At least I hope she did, because initially I didn't like my new nickname. I much preferred the first ten-plus years of my daughter's life when she'd cover my face in kisses or see how hard she could hug me. But I slowly embraced being the "Worst Dad in the World" when I realized it meant I was right where I wanted to be in my parenting.

One of my goals as a dad was to push my kids to achieve beyond what they thought possible without irritating them . . . too much. I don't always walk that line very well, but I'm trying.

There aren't a whole lot of verses aimed directly at fathers in the Bible. But Colossians 3:21 clearly states, "Fathers, do not embitter your children, or they will become discouraged" (NIV). Digging into that verse I found that the Greek word for *embitter* means to provoke or irritate. The key idea is that fathers shouldn't irritate and demotivate their children; instead they should encourage and strengthen them. Sometimes that encouragement includes beef jerky, supportive words and six-mile hikes at altitude.

As my daughter got older, I heard that nickname less and less. Maybe she figured out that I pushed because I loved. And recently, I just got a text from my daughter that read, "You are the bestest dad in the whole world!"

I smiled and started to reply when I received another message. This one, "I didn't write that. Mom did."

Oh well, I'll take what I can get.

Prayer: Dear heavenly Father, help me to love, guide, and encourage my children in the same way You help me. Amen.

∽

Jesse Florea has written more than twenty books and thousands of newspaper and magazine articles. He lives in Colorado Springs with his wife and enjoys hanging out with his two grown children.

He Cried With Me

Courtney Fink

I'm hopeless," I thought sitting in my room. "No one can help me. I want to die."

I'd just opened up to my parents and told them everything I had done. When I finished, I longed for acceptance. Instead, I saw my dad shaking his head in disbelief. I couldn't handle the guilt. Now I sat alone in my room reliving every moment of my childhood.

Born into a dysfunctional family, my biological dad beat my brothers and sexually abused me. My mom was schizophrenic and bi-polar. She'd burst into anger. As a baby, she left me in the bathtub with the water running. I was rescued by a social service worker after I almost drowned. This rescue led to my first experience with foster care.

My family convinced the Court that we were stable and allowed us to leave. Officials placed me into Foster Care after my mom beat my brother relentlessly. My parents still had custody of us, so we were sent back home. My mom blew this chance when she put my brother into a tub of scalding water. After rushing him to the hospital, the police put my mom in jail. They took us from our parents. The Court terminated their rights to have children, so I belonged to the state.

The system passed me to different homes and kicked me out of many. I saw counselors, but only became more hurt and confused, hiding my pain. I was in shelters because no one wanted me. I sought control by stealing money from my foster parents. I wanted to live a normal life, but that chance was gone. A family wanted to adopt me, but I became scared of my dream come true. They changed their minds and dropped me off at a shelter and said I was too "messed-up." That day, first time I was allowed to dream again, I was crushed again and put back into the system.

Several years later, after living in different therapeutic homes, I was at a family reunion when somebody asked, "What do you want for Christmas, Courtney?" I can still hear two godly people asking me this question. I replied, "All I want for Christmas is for a Christian family to adopt me." Those same people had a dream from God; they were supposed to adopt me. I became filled with hope, because I had a family again. Little did they realize who I really was. They taught me about Jesus Who died for my sin. I felt too broken and Jesus could never love me. I lived with secrets. I'd be rejected if I told the truth. One day, I decided to trust my parents and tell them. I was broken inside as I poured out everything.

Still sitting in my room, my mom jerked me back into reality. I told her I hated life and I wanted to die. The next morning, I woke up crying on a stiff, hospital bed. My therapist said the only thing that could help was medication. My parents didn't know how to fix what I had destroyed. I spent a week in the mental hospital. When I left, I came back to the hurt, shame, and guilt I thought was gone. I became more desperate to die. I started hurting myself more. My parents searched hard for help. I was lonely and wanted someone to love me. I could feel them trying to love me through it, yet didn't know what to do.

They found Teen Challenge. When I arrived, I heard testimonies of shattered lives and transformation. I cried hard because I knew Jesus was opening His arms up to me. I knew He loved me no matter what. He knows the pain, secrets, lies, hurts – everything. When He saw me in my room crying, He cried with me. He smiled and knew that my life was going to be transformed, and I would arrive at Teen Challenge and find hope. My family is restored; my life is new.

God knows the good, bad, and the ugly secrets. He gave His life and knew I'd hurt, deny, and push Him away. Feeling the pain of the nails being driven into His hands and the slashes in His back, He thought of me. He doesn't want anyone to feel unworthy of His love.

Prayer: Dear Heavenly Father, You promised never to forsake us— to accept us, knowing who we'll become. We come to you with everything, Father, and know you will do mighty things and heal our wounds. Amen.

❧

Courtney Fink is from Dallas. She's part of Teen Challenge of N.M. sharing Christ's love and healing in churches. She's sixteen, wants to graduate from high school, work for Teen Challenge, and become a worship leader.

He Is Enough

Brianna Joyce

I am plagued with inadequacy. God has seen fit to bless my life with people who love Him, but so often I've felt like less of a Christian than them. Their walk seems strong, their faith seems perfect. And here I am, struggling with doubt and worries. I know that each of us battles our own struggles, but I still I compare myself to others. I am ashamed that I could doubt God. I berate myself for worrying endlessly when the Creator of the Universe watches over me. When God has provided such marvelous gifts, how dare I have the audacity to spurn them? My failures confront me, and I feel defeated.

But God remembers what I am. He knows I am a fallen creature, incapable of existing without wickedness. As every other human, I have it in me to commit horrible deeds. Even my small lies and excuses are nothing but utter filth in comparison to God's unfathomable perfection.

Next to God, my failures are disgusting. Undesirable. Yet despite all this, despite the sin and depravity of every human's sin nature, God sees something in me worth saving. He sees the child made in His image, worth sending His Son to die a terrible death. Would you sacrifice your only child for an undeserving wretch? God did.

I have nothing to offer God, yet He still loves me more than any human ever could. The door was opened by His Son's blood. All I had to do was come as I was. The work was done, the sacrifice made once for all. And so God in His grace reminds me that on my own, I can do nothing. But standing on His shoulders I can rise above my failures, and refuse to be defined by them. When I stumble, His love will not grow sour. I am no longer bound to sin, but freed by the blood of the ultimate sacrifice.

God often has to let us fall before He can build us up. Our old ways must be torn down before we can learn new ones. From where He's brought me, I see how self-centered I am. I find myself thinking *"What if I didn't believe enough? I always worry. I can't do it."* I, I, I. Do you see any mention of God?

But it's not about me. It's not about what I did or didn't do. It's all about what He did—once. God has promised that the blood of Christ is enough for Him. If the God of the universe is satisfied, I can be, too.

In John 10:27-29 Jesus says something incredible.

> My sheep hear my voice, and I know them, and they follow Me. And I give them eternal life, and they shall never perish; neither shall anyone snatch them out of My hand. My Father, who has given them to me, is greater than all; and no one is able to snatch them out of My Father's hand (NKJV)..

Once you trust that Jesus' death is enough for you, you're His. Forever. Yes, that's right. How incredible is that? No matter what you do, where you go, or what happens to you, you will always belong to God.

I can do nothing, but He has done everything.

When you struggle, remember this. You are not saved by your own power, nor can you maintain your salvation by trying to be a perfect Christian. It is done by the power of Christ alone, and He is enough.

Prayer: Heavenly Father, I pray that You will challenge us in our faith. Do what You need to do to bring us closer to You, even if that means breaking us down. Amen.

❧

Brianna Joyce has been writing since she was six and drew a story about a duck on construction paper. She says, "Writing brings me a sense of excitement and completeness that nothing else does. The power of words can transform people, and I want to use their power as God's tool to influence others for Christ."

The Incessant Buzz

Wendy Taryn Deluca

Busy as a bee—that's me. Buzzing from one task to another, in a state of constant activity. Intense, focused, driven, alone. My projects draw me like pollen. Zip, zip, zip, from flower to flower, the bee has to get his quota of nectar for the day. I have to complete today's tasks. All of them. Frenzied. Frazzled. My "to do" list swarms in my head. The noise is deafening.

Unrealistic expectations and unobtainable deadlines keep me from getting everything done. There is always more nectar to carry back to the hive. Overwhelmed, stressed, and irritable, I isolate and put projects before people. Diligence or obsession—where do I draw the line? My behavior is unhealthy, but I can't stop. I am addicted.

A wake-up call came when my mind was preoccupied due to rushing around. I missed getting in a severe car wreck by only inches. It scared me. I realized my life had spun out of control. The land flowing with milk and honey God promised wasn't flooded with stress and anxiety. Things had to change.

I whispered, "Lord, help me! I am overwhelmed. My mind always buzzes, making me dizzy. I circle around and don't know where to land.

Make it stop! Your Word says to come just as I am. My personality is analytical, detail oriented, and organized, sometimes to the extreme. I obsess with whatever task I am working on, and relationships with others suffer. How can this be used for Your glory?

Breakthrough came when I felt God quiet my mind and speak to my spirit. "Yes, this is who you are. I have wired you for My purpose. Seek me first and I will show you," (Matthew 6:33, paraphrased). The Lord was calling me to intimacy with Him, but I missed out due to self-inflicted busyness. My heart made a beeline back to God. He is the first flower to visit, to drink of His nectar. Then He will enable me to get the things done that He needs me to do. God will help me stay grounded, not hovering in mid air.

How do I build my life around Him and not a "to do" list? All the time and money I spent on college never taught me the life lesson of balance. Surprisingly, my analytical mind had the answer. Commit the day to God and let Him organize my agenda and set priorities. Trust that He has a better plan for me than I have for myself. The result is a quiet time spreadsheet I designed with daily goals, prayers, scriptures, and reflections. Not a task to complete, but an act of worship from my heart to His, tapping into the unique gifts He has given me.

Slowing down is a daily struggle. The enemy wants to distract me with unimportant busywork. I surrender this to God with my left-brained solution: post-it notes that say "Is this really what you need to be doing right now?" plastered all over my house. On the bathroom mirror, refrigerator, kitchen table, computer…

As I grow closer in intimacy with God, He reminds me of an important blossom I sometimes miss: people. In order to love my neighbors as myself, I have to stop writing them out of my schedule. When I am not focused on my own agenda, it's more natural for me to see the needs of others. It's not just about me, but all of us working together. Spending a few extra minutes eating with coworkers instead of locked in my office in front of the computer may result in blessings I would have otherwise missed.

The bee gathers pollen and then returns to the hive. He lives a balance of solitary work and time spent in community. As a Christian, I want to find a balance of connection and fellowship with people, but also time alone with the Lord. Then I can tune out the hum to hear God's gentle whisper about tasks He assigned me and people He put in my path. His words entice me. They are sweeter than honey. (See Psalm 119:103.)

Prayer: Lord, help me be still. Show me what You want me to do today. Establish my steps and lead me away from activities that distract from Your will. Help me make time to connect with others and give a word of encouragement. If I am overwhelmed, may it be by Your love, mercy, and grace. I pray in Jesus' name, Amen.

Wendy Taryn Deluca, a U.S. Navy Veteran and Clinical Therapist providing faith-based counseling, studied at Liberty University and Australia's Hillsong International Leadership College. For more information she can be contacted at nolessthangodsbest@gmail.com, www.nolessthangodsbest.com or facebook.com/nolessthangodsbest.

Too Dumb to Be a Missionary?

Kathy Hall

L ife was a little crazy around our house. The Home Mission Board had appointed my husband and me to evangelize gang members, drug addicts, alcoholics, and other troubled people in a ministry called Teen Challenge. Sometimes they lived with us.

One day in the fall, I had my own two teenaged girls to get ready, a twelve-year old whose mother was in rehab for heroin addiction, a fifteen-year-old girl who had just gotten out of drug rehab, and a four-teen-year old girl whose mother had just been murdered. They were all dressed, fed, beds made, devotions done, dishes finished, and the house was put back together. I got them all to school on time, and my husband and a young man on probation got to the office alive!

Despite suffering from a terrible cold, after everyone got where they were headed, I went to my office for an hour, then returned home to open the door for Joe, the piano tuner, a man from our church. When he was just about finished, he wrapped up his tools and I sat down near him to be hospitable. My lips and nose were very chapped, so I grabbed mentholatum and rubbed it really good all over my lips and nose. Oh, it felt so good. I smeared on a little more. Joe finished up and I showed him to the door.

I decided to check my makeup before returning to the office.

"O no! There's lipstick all over my face!" I cried when I saw that the mentholatum that felt so good on my chapped lips and nose had smeared my lipstick everywhere. I was so embarrassed. How would I ever show my face in church? Joe probably laughed all the way to his car. He sat there and watched me but never said a word about the mess I made on my face. Why didn't he say something?

I felt completely stupid. Why would the Lord trust me to do His work when I didn't even know I made a fool of myself? How could I speak at the next women's event coming up? Or represent the ministry of Teen Challenge on television?

"Lord, how can You use *me*? I'm such a mess. How can anyone so dumb be a missionary?"

Joe never mentioned the lipstick all over my face to anyone—that I know of. The "lipstick story" taught me how many times I fail and don't even see it, but God and other people do. Though they don't tell me, they still see I'm a mess.

I came to God a mess. In some ways I'm still a mess. It is by God's grace, love, and mercy He uses me. Not because I'm "good enough." He sees all my messes, all my failures, all my shortcomings, all my sins, and He loves me anyway. He loves me so much that while I was yet a sinner He gave His life for me. Tears fill my eyes, and my heart is overwhelmed with humility to know His love for me is unfailing.

In Psalm 19:12(NIV), David said, "But who can discern their own errors? Forgive my hidden faults." The lipstick story is about a small mess, but I've made some really big messes in my life. Some I know about and many I don't. I am so thankful to know He won't embarrass me; I do a good job of that all by myself.

Prayer: Lord Jesus, please forgive me all my sin, known and unknown. Thank You for Your mercy and grace. It's Your grace that makes me "good enough" to serve You. In Your name I pray, Amen.

❧

Kathy Hall and her husband have helped troubled people find

freedom through Jesus Christ in the ministry Teen Challenge for more than thirty years. She is a certified Advanced Personality Trainer. Kathy wants everyone to know, love, and serve Jesus Christ.

The Awakening

Aaron M. Zook, Jr.

Like a fat caterpillar, I spent the first eighteen years of my life munching away, feeding on my parents and the world around me. My father's U.S. Air Force career moved us frequently in the United States and to international environments in Japan, The Netherlands, and Germany. My mother worked financial positions and often served as church organist and choir director. I had two sisters and one brother. Mom and Dad attended a liturgical church, which became the faith-basis of my spiritual upbringing. I soaked in these unique experiences, coasting through life.

I breezed through school with ease, sang in choirs, and played guitar. I didn't fit in with the popular folks at school—I was a loner. When I was fourteen years old, I thought I would become a pastor. However, during my first college year at Penn State, my life changed drastically.

I walked away from my spiritual upbringing and convictions. I struck out on a new path, a journey without church, the Bible, or Christian friends. My philosophy included God because He is everywhere, but not organized religion with its rules and restrictions. I spun strands of selfishness, encasing myself in a cocoon of human wisdom and friendship instead of God's.

The strands became cords wrapping me tighter in the chrysalis, intertwining with poor decisions to squeeze the breath out of my life. I drank alcohol heavily, gambled, chased after attractive women, and partied in my free time. In spite of my poor judgment, social decline, and moral blunders, bright patches of light visible through the shell's thin sections kept me going. I served four years of enlisted Air Force service, sang and danced in the Okinawa Choral Society, and met and romanced my wife, Joyce. But these good things didn't wake me and create an urge to escape; they lulled me into accepting a dim and darkening future.

Joyce brought light into my world, inspiring me to change some of my ways. I reduced my swearing, drinking, and other carousing. I became a one-woman man. I returned with her to Penn State to finish my college degree and we got married. While I was in college, Joyce searched for something to fill the emptiness in her life that I couldn't satisfy. She committed her life to Jesus Christ through a TV evangelist show.

The sparks began to fly in our house! The dimness inside the comfortable cocoon became unbearable blackness as God intruded into my life again. I couldn't talk about it. I demanded Joyce stop watching TV evangelists.

Joyce submitted. Being a new Christian, she told me she needed to go to church. I agreed. Eventually, unknown to me, Joyce had the members of her new church praying for my soul. She invited me to attend a dinner with her small Bible study group, telling me to avoid an older man, Ed Hoch, a spiritual elder.

But, confident I knew more than enough about God and the Bible, I made a beeline for Ed when I entered the house. Ed listened patiently and his answers intrigued me. I decided to attend the church and Bible studies to learn more. Even though my previous path had brought some disastrous results, I realized God could wipe the slate clean. Instead of traveling a shadowy road leading to an eternal life of pain and terror, I could submit to a loving God who would forgive me for all I had done.

I woke up. I broke out of the cocoon and turned everything I am over to God through Jesus Christ. One night, on top of a Pennsylvanian mountain, I confessed to God that I fell short of His standards. I was wrong—wrong about Him, wrong about being able to live His absolute values alone, and wrong about what gave life meaning.

It's amazing what changes God has made in me. I am free of guilt and shame. I've spread my wings, learning how to fly in His beautiful light and breathe deeply the joy of life. Jesus united my wife and me as one, gave me a forever family of Christian brothers and sisters, and lifted me to spectacular heights of keener insight. What more could I do in thanks than dedicate myself to helping others to wake up and break out of their chrysalis, emerging into the freedom of being in Christ.

Prayer: Lord, wake me up to the spiritual reality of my life and this world. Forgive my past mistakes, bad decisions, and failures. Create in me a clean heart focused on You. Amen.

❧

Aaron M. Zook, Jr., Colonel, U.S. Army (Retired), writes a

Young Adult mystery/adventure series. Find his books at Amazon.com and ZookBooks.org. Like him at Facebook.com/ZookBooks. Aaron and his wife, Joyce, have two married sons.

The Love of the Father

Jennifer Smith

Behold what manner of love the Father has bestowed on us,
that we should be called children of God! (1 John 1:3 NIV).

For years I assumed I was going to heaven. I knew the gospel of
Jesus Christ. God became man and came to earth to save mankind
from their sins. For the most part this gospel didn't affect how I lived
my life.

I thought I was a pretty good person anyway. Although I grew up going
to church and Catholic school, I left that behind as an adult. By the
world's standards I was doing well. I had a good family, a good job,
and was a law-abiding contributing member of society. Something in
me longed for something more. As a risk taker, I had experimented
with drugs in my youth, so getting involved in meth in my mid-
twenties didn't seem like a big deal. The drugs sped up my production
and helped my social skills. Drugs seemed a positive thing in my life.

It wasn't long though before I was hooked and I cried out to God for
deliverance. I had no knowledge about grace, so I thought I needed to

clean myself up—then I'd be acceptable to God. I made promises to God to quit but my love of the drugs got the better of me. Sin had me trapped on the roller coaster of despair.

In the years that followed, I would lose many things—my house, boat, vehicle. But nothing prepared me for the loss of my beloved father. When I received the news that he died unexpectedly at the age of 54, in anguish I fell to my knees and told God, "I'll never be able to clean myself up now."

In hindsight I can see how true Romans 8:28 was in the situation. My dad's death was the worst thing that ever happened, yet it was the catalyst that brought me to the place of admitting I could never clean myself up. In my grief I could only turn to God. I drew close to the Lord in my grief and stopped making promises to Him. I stopped trying to perform and make myself acceptable to Him. I began listening to the Christian radio station for comfort and for the first time heard teachers who were real people talking about a personal relationship with God through Jesus.

I began to understand grace and the Father's love for me just as I am. In a watershed moment, I realized that if my dad could have died to set me free from the tyranny of meth he would have done so. His love for me was unconditional. In that moment the Lord spoke to my heart and said, *someone did die to set you free and it wasn't your dad, it was Jesus.* One year and three months after my dad's death, I took the step of faith and threw away the drugs that had been a part of my daily existence for years. In the eleven years since, Jesus has become my life and my love, and restored to me all that was lost. I have been embraced and transformed by the love of my heavenly Father.

My experience shows that anyone who belongs to Christ has become a new person. The old life is gone; a new life has begun! All these life-truths are a gift from God, who brought us back to himself through Christ. And God has given us this task of reconciling people to him. For God was in Christ, reconciling the world to himself, no longer counting people's sins against them. And he gave us this wonderful message of reconciliation. So we are Christ's ambassadors; God is making his appeal through us. We speak for Christ when we plead, "Come back to God!"

> For God made Christ, who never sinned, to be the offering
> for our sin, so that we could be made right with God through
> Christ (2 Corinthians 5:17-21 NLT).

Prayer: Heavenly Father, thank you for your pursuit, your love, and your transforming grace. Thank you for fulfilling and satisfying me in ways that the things of this world never could. Amen.

Jennifer Smith is a new creation in Christ called out of darkness into His glorious light. She is a writer, speaker, and Bible teacher living in Albuquerque NM with her husband Steve.

Meeting Daddy

Cynthia Ruchti

My father served with the Marines during the Korean Conflict. Four days after I was born, his unit shipped out, leaving my mom and me to fend for ourselves for the next thirteen months. When relating my personal history, I have to start with that story. It shaped my beginnings. I lived my first thirteen months seven thousand miles away from the dad who loved me and wasn't allowed to hold me until I was already walking and capable of squirming out of his arms.

Fathers weren't welcome in the delivery room in those days. He saw his first glimpses of me through the nursery window. Then he obediently reported for duty aboard the ship that would take him far from us and into the arms of daily danger. In an era before the invention of camcorders, camera phones, and e-mail, my mother and father had only airmail letters to connect their hearts. Letters and scalloped-edged, black-and-white photos.

As the firstborn child, my photo album bulged, all the more so since still pictures offered my dad his only tangible evidence that I was alive, growing, and as happy as a child can be without her father.

When I learned to blow kisses, Mom would "collect" some in an envelope to send to him. An amateur artist, Daddy sketched cartoonish scenes from his Marine unit—jeeps and tents and enlisted men and helicopters. Even before I understood a word she said, my mom read those letters to me. They were my lullabies. She showed me his picture and talked about what a wonderful daddy I had.

Mom wanted me to know who he was and what he was like before he came home. From the stories they've told, both my parents were nervous about that first meeting. They worried I'd be frightened of the stranger who was my father. He'd survived the war, but my fearing or resisting him would have killed him, they said.

To compound the concern, I was at that age when a toddler begins to fear strangers. Somebody would smile at me in church and I'd start screaming.

But my mom had prepared me well. The pictures. The letters. Her gentle words about how much that smiling man in the pictures loved me. When he finally came home and walked through the front door, I looked at my mom, pointed to the tall Marine, and asked, "Daddy?" Her nod was all the assurance I needed. The next minute I was in his arms, dodging his tears of gratitude that I'd accepted him.

My toddler mind entertained no doubt that he cared about me. I knew that truth before he even got home from the war because of what my mother taught me about him.

If the Lord walked into the room right now, would the people around me recognize Him not by His beard or flowing robes, but because of how I have described Him?

Would people meeting Him for the first time find the situation comfortable and reassuring because of how well I prepared them? Am I constantly showing others snapshots of the Lord through the way I live and love, the things I say about Him, the things He said that I pass on to them? Would His sudden Presence seem intimidating and frightening, or more like a warm homecoming?

In light of how you and I act day today, would others respond to His entrance into their lives this way:

"Oh, sure! I recognize Him. I've heard my neighbor talk about Him. I've seen my coworker act like that. I've heard those same affirming words coming out of my brother-in-law's mouth. I've seen examples of what He's like. His amazing love and generosity and compassion and caring don't surprise me at all. They are just what I expected from what my friend shared about Him. I heard that His touch brings healing. I heard that He can help make sense out of the questions that trouble me. I didn't need more of an introduction than the one my friend already gave me. I'd recognize Jesus a mile away."

Prayer: Lord God, we want to represent You well to a world that doesn't yet know You. Thank You for giving us a story worth telling, about a Father's love worth embracing without hesitation. Amen.

∽

Cynthia Ruchti is an award-winning author and speaker who

tells stories hemmed in hope, drawing from three decades writing for Christian radio. She serves as the Professional Relations Liaison for American Christian Fiction Writers. www.cynthiaruchti.com.

Just As I Am?

Carole Klock

Come as you are? I am not good enough.

When I was growing up, I was told over and over how inept I was; how very flawed. I couldn't do anything right, I would never amount to anything.

If I received a call today inviting me to a "Come As You Are" party, I'd run into the bathroom, fix my makeup, change my shirt, and get cleaned up.

If I wanted to go before my Heavenly Father, I'd have to "clean myself up" first. I wouldn't go to church unless I was dressed properly. I remember with a chuckle the first time my adult daughter saw her mother wear pants to church. Her startled reaction was comical. However, I am just beginning to learn what my Lord means when He encourages me to come to Him just as I am.

This change did not come easily. I had to go through a deep personal valley to understand that my Father cares for me in every circumstance of my life. I can't make myself good enough. He has declared me good enough to come to Him at any time.

In July 2013, my husband and I lost our oldest son to cancer. I have never known such pain and sorrow. I was completely broken.

When Tom entered the hospital for the last time, I knew it was close to the end. After several days, we took him home with Hospice. The family set up a vigil around the clock.

I remember being calm and unemotional. "I don't' understand this; I should be falling apart here," I thought. "Why am I so together?" Then it hit me; my Father promised to meet my need. He promised me His peace. I didn't feel peaceful. My heart was breaking. I knew my son was dying. Yet, I remained calm. I found strength I never knew I had. God was keeping His promise.

Grief had never come so near to me. After his death was over and life resumed, I was surprised at how normal I seemed. I went to church. I attended choir rehearsal and sang on Sunday mornings as usual. I went to my quilt club meetings and to writers' group. I continued with all the normal activities of my life. Harry and I went back our job, managing a self- storage facility.

It was all a sham.

I assumed I'd grieve for a period of time. Then I'd simply move on. I was wrong. The grief came right along with me as I resumed my life. That's when I realized I had no heart for cleaning myself up or getting myself prepared to enter the presence of my Lord. I needed my Father desperately. In that desperation, I dashed into His throne room crying,

"Daddy, Daddy, help me." Sometimes I was driving and pulled off the road. Other times I couldn't see. I'd crumble in a heap on the floor or the bed and just let the emotion wash over me.

I sensed no fancy worded prayers or organized quiet times. Only His child groping in the dark for her Father's loving arms. At no time was I not received, welcomed, and comforted by my Lord. When the tears came, they just came. In Sunday service when a hymn touched my aching heart, I simply let the tears flow.

I learned I can hide nothing from my Lord. He already knows. My faith is stronger. I have heard people say they're stronger when a loved one dies, but now I have experienced it. I trust Jesus more than ever. God is good!

Prayer: Psalm 59:16 (ESV) "But I will sing of your strength; I will sing aloud of your steadfast love in the morning. For you have been to me a fortress and a refuge in the day of my distress." Amen.

Carole Klock has been married to Harry 57 years. They have a son, a daughter, seven grandkids and five greats. She enjoys reading, writing, quilting, singing, and taking care of Miniature Schnauzers; especially one named Allie.

When God Smiles

Shauna L. Hoey

As a teacher, I oversaw the playground. My eyes were drawn to Erin, crouched down in the shade with her dress spread out around her legs. Her china doll face and white blonde hair caught my attention as she crunched the rock-hard dirt with her shovel. Erin immersed herself in the moment, captivated by the wonder of dirt. Time stopped as I became aware of the sweetness of this beautiful little girl and how God must delight in her. I walked over and sat next to her and said, "You make God smile, Erin."

Later, the same day I felt arms wrap around my legs and squeeze me with all their might, and then release quickly. I looked round and saw a dust cloud from little Erin running away as fast as she could. Erin is a free spirit who doesn't fit the mold. She is like a hummingbird darting from one place to another dancing to her own music in her own time. Her big hug was a connection I cherished. I saw the child that God sees, and she must have felt His love through my eyes.

I wonder how God delights in my uniqueness. If I saw myself through His eyes of adoration, what would I notice? What makes God smile in my life even when I leave dust cloud behind me?

Prayer: Dear Lord, allow me to see myself through Your eyes and feel Your love. Help me slow down long enough to behold Your vision of those around me. May I see through Your eyes and make others feel Your smile today. Amen

> The LORD your God is with you, he is mighty to save. He will take great delight in you, he will quiet you with his love, he will rejoice over you with singing (Zephaniah 3:17 NIV).

∽

Shauna L. Hoey lives in Manitou Springs with her husband and two teenagers. Her passion is communicating God's Truth so others flourish in their purpose.

The Accident

Kim D. Mullaney

It should have been a fatal crash for all six occupants: my husband, four of our children, and me. Our Suburban was traveling at 65 mph, when I reached for my purse. The handle was caught. As I tugged on it, my arm jerked, and the right front tire veered off the asphalt. I tried to maneuver back onto the pavement. Suddenly our car slammed into a cement post and flipped end-over-end. We landed upside down on an embankment. Next, the Suburban rolled repeatedly side-over-side through the dirt median and across the on-coming traffic lanes.

Because we had left early that morning, everyone wanted to sleep. For comfort, they each took off their seat belts. What a costly decision. Two of our family members were thrown through the shattered windows: my husband Mark onto the asphalt and our youngest son Kenneth onto the desert sand. Our three other children—Kevin, Matthew, and Kristin—had been tossed about inside the car, amid luggage, loosed carjacks, and each other's precious lives. I was the only one belted-in, clinging in futility to the steering wheel, desperately pleading, "Father God, no! Father God, no! Father God, no!"

Within seconds Matthew climbed out of the wreckage and pulled Kristin out through a broken window. He yelled to Kevin and me, "Get out! Get away from the Suburban!"

I climbed through the missing passenger window and ran to Mark. I knelt beside him, cradling his bleeding head. I cried out, "Father God, You gave Mark to me. He is Yours. You did not bring us here to die! You alone, Father, are faithful and true!" Even though I had been the one driving, I never questioned if God heard or rejected my declarations of trust. I simply knew that He was trustworthy.

Questions mounted. Is Mark alive? Why is Kenneth crying? How do I get help? We are alone in the Mexican desert. Are the rest of my children really okay? How do I get my family to a hospital in the US? Where is the money going to come from? How do I get news to our oldest son Mark Louis who is still at home in Monterrey, Mexico?

God was my only hope. He never left me. Often fears, decisions, and questions challenged me. Each time, God filled my heart with strength, love, and assurance.

Just one week later, I found myself in a restaurant, basking in the presence of my children. I marveled that we were all alive, together for the first time since the accident. Mark was stable, still in the hospital, and had survived both the wreck and three major surgeries. Kenneth received two surgeries and had been released. Kevin, Matthew, Kristin, and I had sustained only minor injuries. Precious miracles.

Suddenly without warning, the tangible essence of God's Presence flooded my very being. I heard Him say, "Your definition of perfection is not the same as mine! The cross was seen by many as a complete failure. Yet, on the other side past the cross was My 'Most Perfect' act since creation. Everything that would ever need to be redeemed was stamped: 'Paid in Full!' In your lives, on the other side of this accident, is My 'More Perfect' will."

I had been the one driving… I was the one responsible… Even so, our God suddenly burst into this moment with His love and clarity. He received me and embraced me, just as I was, knowing exactly what was required for my healing, forgiveness, and journey.

"As for God, His way is perfect; The word of the Lord is proven; He is a shield to all who trust in Him. For who is God, except the Lord? And who is a rock, except our God? It is God who arms me with strength, and makes my way perfect" (Psalm 18: 30-32 NKJV).

Prayer: Dear God, You truly are our only hope in time of need. Thank You for Your faithfulness, guidance, and "More Perfect" will. Thank You that our lives are stamped, "Paid in Full." Amen.

❧

Kim D. Mullaney is a wife, mother, and grandmother. She serves as a missionary, children's and women's minister, teacher, home group leader, and TV co-host with her husband, Dr. Mark Mullaney, at Jesus First Transformation Warehouse in Albuquerque, New Mexico.

Perfection or Willingness?

LuAnn Edwards

May the God of peace…equip you with everything good for doing his will, and may he work in us what is pleasing to him, through Jesus Christ, to whom be glory for ever and ever. Amen (Hebrews 13: 20-21 NIV).

I stood upon this verse a couple of years ago when asked to sing a lengthy solo with the choir. Other choir members could have done a better job singing, but I felt strongly the Lord wanted me to sing this particular song. Unfortunately, I had recently lost my voice.

Before this, I had only sung a few small solos. I had been praying for the Lord to allow me the opportunity to sing a song that truly would bless the congregation. It was my heart's desire to allow the Holy Spirit to use me in reaching hurting people. This solo was a new song for me; however, as I listened to it for the first time I knew without a doubt this was the answer to my prayers. This song of hope ministered to me in many ways and moved me to tears. Although I had no voice, how could I possibly say no to something I had prayed and asked the Lord to do?

I had ten days to get ready to sing. Surely the Lord would heal me so I could bring Him glory. I prayed, I fasted, I prayed and prayed some more. No healing came. My voice was in such poor shape I wasn't even able to practice the song. I was only able to listen to it and sing it in my heart.

Hebrews 13:21 says God will equip me with everything good for doing His will, and because I believed it was His will for me to sing this solo, I believed He would equip me to sing.

That Sunday morning, I took a step of faith, knowing I could easily have been humiliated. Also, I didn't want my voice to interfere with the message of hope and healing in the song; the words to "Where Joy and Sorrow Meet" were moving.

Another soloist was available to sing if I could not; however, I felt the Lord confirming this was what He wanted me to do, to trust Him fully. As I left my place in the choir to take center stage, I prayed one more time asking the Holy Spirit to take over; in myself, I had nothing to give.

After singing, several from the choir told me the solo was beautiful. One choir member even said it made her cry. I believe the Holy Spirit sang through me that Sunday morning. I came before Him just as I was—not at all good enough, but totally yielded to Him and willing to honor and praise Him as I sang. I believe He accomplished what He intended that day and He was pleased. Was it perfection? No, but He took my willingness, and I truly believe His anointing was upon me in a very special way.

God equips us; He does not expect us to act on our own. He gives us everything good to do His will. He works in us what is pleasing to Him through Jesus Christ. It is our place to give Him access to our hearts, lives, and gifts or talents He has given us. We do not have to come to Him in perfection. We must simply come! He will take what we offer and do a marvelous work in and through us!

What is the Lord asking you to do for Him? Pray and ask Him to help you accept His calling; be willing to allow Him to equip you to carry out His plan.

Prayer: Father, thank you for accepting me as I am—imperfections and all. Help me be willing to be led by Your Spirit and allow You to work in and through my life. Amen.

❧

LuAnn Edwards and her husband Kenn live in Albuquerque, New Mexico. They have two adult children, a teenaged daughter, and three beautiful grandchildren. She enjoys reading, writing, hiking, and spending time with her family.

A Preacher is Born

Scott Payne

I'm the hero of my stories, so why would I not stand before God with confidence in the masterpiece of me?

The rising sun announced my birth to a respected family that lived in a small town. My father, a professional man and gifted manager, held me that Sunday and proclaimed, "This boy will be a preacher." Handing me back to the nurse, Dad made his way to church. He taught Sunday school, which took precedence over everything else.

I knew my destiny from birth, and my parents encouraged it. They kept the Bible before my eyes. Church attendance became a multi-weekly event. If the doors were open, we were there.

I can remember only one time when I questioned my place in the Kingdom of God and that was simply a misunderstanding between a preschooler and his teacher.

Dora told the class one day that there would be no pains in heaven. Being four years old, with a last name Payne, set me up for an emotional crisis I didn't give Dora a chance to resolve. Bolting out of the classroom, I headed straight to my mother. She would set Dora straight.

The rest of my childhood was lived out in that small church with a doting mother, loving father, supportive family, and encouraging friends. In fact, the blessings of my life continued to enhance my role in the Kingdom of God, which culminated in my prayer as an eighteen-year-old senior, kneeling by my bed one night.

"Dear God, You are the creator of the universe, and I will do anything and go anywhere You want me to go. In Jesus's name. Amen."

Four hour later, I woke up covered in sweat, dealing with the worst case of the what-if's that pulled me out of bed and back to my knees.

"What if God doesn't want me to get married? What if God doesn't want me to drive a nice car? What if He wants me to be a missionary in Africa? What if He wants me to work with the homeless? Dear God, I will work for You. I will be a minister for You, but I will take care of the details. In Jesus' name I pray. Amen." Satisfied with my dedication, commitment, and clarification with God, I climbed back into bed worry free.

The next eight months flew by. As senior class president owning the fastest car in town, I had it made. Then I broke my wrist, lost my summer job, sold my car, and found out when I went to Bible college that God had called hundreds of young people to be His messengers.

My parents were wrong. I'm not a one-and-only in the Kingdom of God. I'm one of many and did not know how to process that thought.

My parents raised me to believe in the wonder of me, my special abilities, and my place in God's Kingdom, but provided little preparation to deal with the wonder of others. At college, the struggle for identity became a daily battle. I did not understand what happened and I could not talk with my parents since they were having their own set of marital problems.

With all the blessings gone that I had bathed in for years, suicide seemed an option. Then sitting in a dark theater at a Second Chapter of Acts concert trying to comprehend what went wrong in my life, the bus driver for the group walked out on stage. With his guitar, he started singing about Humpty Dumpty.

He told the whole story on my life. The pride, the arrogance, the wall upon which I sat and fell. In that three minute song, my Heavenly Father laid open my life, reminding me of my prayer one year earlier. Now, He was asking me, if I wanted to follow Him, no strings attached. All I could do was cry.

Back in the dorm room later that night, my Heavenly Father led me to the opening phrase of the greatest sermon given to humanity. Matthew 5:3 says, "Blessed are the poor in spirit, for theirs is the kingdom of heaven (KJV)." In those simple but profound words, my Heavenly Father began the process that melted my arrogance into His holy poverty.

Prayer: Dear Heavenly Father, please be the author of my stories. Give me the wisdom to know what to do and the courage to do it. Amen.

❦

Communicating the wonders of God's love drives **Scott Payne** to explore writing as one more tool he can use to reach those longing to find joy and peace.

The Perfect Way of Imperfection

Neema Anderson

From a young age I was surrounded by stories from the Bible filled with brilliance: Godly men and women standing up for their faith and being excellent role models. My personal role model was Paul. I saw a devoted follower of Christ who could do no wrong. I wanted to harness the perfection I thought he held.

As I grew up, I started to see all the imperfections inside me. I learned to hold back everything imperfect about me. I did not want to be torn down or seen as less than what was expected.

Have you ever felt shameful of your imperfections? I even tried to hide my imperfections from God. I knew I wasn't actually hiding from God, but the distance was avoidance at its best. I thought that if I could act as though I wasn't broken, needy, and lonely I wouldn't be those things.

The strange thing about avoidance is that it never works. I came face to face with God during a worship service at a youth camp. I had nowhere to hide my imperfections and sin. No time to fix the things I didn't want God to see. I had to choose between walking away, remaining in my broken frail state, or running to God begging him to fix me. I knew that the perfection I wanted to accomplish was impossible.

Then I remembered not just Paul's seemingly-perfect actions, but also the times he was imperfect. I remembered the time, before Paul was a Christian, when he killed Christians and was the farthest from the godly man I idolized. I remembered his fear when he came face to face with God.

Suddenly I realized I didn't have to wait for perfection. I could go to God just as I was, imperfections and all. During that worship service I gave up my search for perfection and began my pursuit of God.

Prayer: O God, thank you for accepting my imperfect brokenness. You are the ultimate healer and forgiver. I am in desperate need of you every day. Amen.

❧

Neema Anderson is a seventeen-year-old senior and aspiring writer from Albuquerque, New Mexico. She is a contributing author to *Life and Learning in the International District*, published in 2014.

The Sweetness of God's Presence

Kenn Edwards

It's almost 9:00 p.m. and down deep inside, you feel it again. You can't explain it, but it happens. Almost like clockwork. Every night that craving strikes again. At first, you fight the urge, but then…

As you open the door to the freezer you see a vast array of delicious ice cream. Your mouth begins to water as you think about different flavors. After all, ice cream each evening has become a habit. Not that it is a bad habit, as long as you watch your caloric intake. But that habit means every day you will want ice cream, knowing very well that you will have that craving again the next day.

God longs for us to have that same kind of craving in our relationship with Him. Much like the late night ice cream snacks, God wants us to spend time with Him every day, too.

Many years ago my life took a new direction. I realized that being good was not enough. For years I had relied on my church membership, my baptism and my good works, to bring me into a right relationship with God. Then I learned that God wanted a deeper personal relationship with me. It was only when I accepted Him into my life as my personal Savior that I became His child.

It doesn't matter who you are or where you have been. God longs for you to love Him and have a relationship with Him. You can know God personally and experience spiritual growth in your life. Just come to the Cross of Christ and spend time with Him every day.

The Psalmist David said, "...I shall seek You earnestly; My soul thirsts for You, my flesh yearns for You, In a dry and weary land where there is no water" (Psalm 63:1 NASB).

Living in a desert has given me a new appreciation to the meaning of a dry and weary land. Unless you are near a water source like a stream or river, nothing will grow. Near the river you will find beautiful farmland, horse farms, and flowering trees that bloom for most of the season. But once you get a half mile from the water, everything dries up.

Like the water for the trees, the nourishment we need to grow in our relationship with God comes from spending time with Him. Disciplines like communicating with God in prayer, studying God's Word, and learning to walk under the influence of the Holy Spirit are all part of growing in Christ. When you seek God every day, you can enjoy a daily refilling of His Spirit.

What happens when we miss our time with God? At first there is a hunger, and we feel that gnawing ache on the inside. Throughout time, if we take no action toward that hunger, it will eventually fade. Just like a dry desert, our fellowship with God will dry up, too—either because we're allowing other things to take God's place in our lives or we've allowed sin to creep into our spirits.

Find the place in your life where you can enjoy the sweet cream of God's Presence. He wants to be a part of your life every day. Work on the daily habit of prayer and Bible study so you can be rejuvenated with the Spirit of God. Be on your guard and watch out, because the things of this life can easily interfere with our intimate time with God.

Seek His counsel daily as you walk with Him. Listen for His voice when it is quiet. Allow His Spirit to influence every aspect of your life, and enjoy a little ice cream as you spend time with God tonight.

Prayer: Father, help me to encounter you every day of my life. Fill my heart with your Spirit so my life will reflect your love to those around me. Amen.

෫

Kenn Edwards is a speaker, author, and financial coach. His background is a combination of financial planning, estate planning, and ministry. Currently he serves with Faith Comes By Hearing in their estate-and-gift-design ministry.

I Believe

John Healton

For His anger lasts only a moment, but his favor lasts a
lifetime; weeping may remain for a night, But rejoicing
comes in the morning (Psalm 30:5 NIV).

Remember Moses' striking the rock out of anger? Peter cutting off
the guard's ear when they came to arrest Jesus? And even Jesus
showing his anger in the temple? My friends, have you ever had an
angry moment, when you just couldn't hold your anger in? I have, and
when that moment came, the first thing I did was to go to the Lord in
prayer. I know this works because I believe in Him.

Because I went to Him first, before I could finish asking Him for
forgiveness, He had already forgiven me. And what a wonderful
feeling that is, to know that even though I showed anger against my
fellow man, God loved me enough to forgive me. Go to Him and He
will be there for you, if you believe in Him.

I have been in many situations, serious ones and minor ones, and each
time I have asked God for His help. Each time, He has been there. I

feel the reason He has helped me so many times is that He wants me to witness to nonbelievers about what He has done in my life. Paul says in Romans 12:13, "Share with God's people who are in need. Practice hospitality" (NIV). Help change the nonbelievers to believers so they too can tell someone that they now believe in Him.

God has helped me with my anger situation, and He has helped me in other situations. When I am in these situations, I know all I have to do is turn to Him for help. Turning to Him is all you have to do also. I walk now with a smile from ear to ear because I believe.

Prayer: Father in Heaven, work with me, mold me into the person you want me to be. Father, be with everyone who, like me, is fighting Satan and give us the power to say, "Satan get behind me in the name of the Father, Son, and Holy Spirit." I believe in you. I thank you now for what you are about to do. Amen.

∽

John Healton loves writing encouraging articles and is working on his first historical Christian fiction book.

The Truth Within the Lie

Larry Crossett

You lied to me," I said. "This isn't a homeless shelter."

Scott Payne, executive director of Inner City Mission, a residential homeless shelter in Springfield, Illinois, had just spent several hours helping me get to know his ministry. Now we sat on the front stoop of the sturdy, time-worn red-brick building, watching neighborhood squirrels gather acorns for the coming winter.

A freelance newspaper journalist, I had approached the pastor after hearing him speak at our church. I was working on a series of profiles of community leaders and wanted to enlist him. He agreed to sit for an interview only on the condition that I first took the time to truly learn about his ministry. He didn't want a superficial review.

I arrived that morning with a pad of paper and backpack full of assumptions: I expected a cold institutional building with rows of cots housing bleak, directionless people. Religious tracts would be littering the floor, along with Gideon Bibles and a whole lot of offensive odors.

Instead, I found giggling children playing in the leaves while their mothers held a Bible study on the back porch. I walked through a kitchen, where several residents worked together preparing supper. Attached to that was a living room, where an older couple sat relaxing on the sofa while a younger woman, somewhat emaciated, talked animatedly on the phone. Instead of the dour faces of downtrodden people, I heard laughter and felt a palpable feeling of joy and optimism.

Still a neophyte Christian, I could not put a name to that feeling. It soon was explained to me: "That's the love of God," a one-time resident, now serving as shelter supervisor, told me.

Next, we ventured to the office building next-door, where I was to attend a staff meeting. I wondered if the "love of God" I had witnessed in the shelter would evaporate as soon as the meeting got underway. Today a resident was being called to account for having come in the previous night drunk and hostile—two conditions prohibited by the rules.

Here was a young lady whose life was in such chaos she couldn't support herself or her kids, facing the people who were doing that job for her—all the way up to the shelter's executive director. Yet, no one took advantage of this perfect opportunity to puff up and act superior. No one pounded on the rule book; no one suggested throwing the woman out on the street to maintain order. Listening to the strict but compassionate instruction this woman received after she spoke on her own behalf, I remember wishing I could discipline my daughter with as much wisdom, love, and respect.

Before the resident was excused from the room, a prayer was offered up. It wasn't, "Lord, help this woman get her act together." It was, "Lord, thank you for (name) and help us to know what is needed in her life."

Now that the tour had finished, Scott asked his question: "What do you think?"

"This isn't a homeless shelter," I said, already plotting out what I wanted to write. "These people *have* a home. They just need places to live."

> For we know that if the earthly tent we live in is destroyed,
> we have a building from God, an eternal house in heaven,
> not built by human hands (2 Corinthians 5:1 NIV).

Prayer: Lord, I pray for the homeless—those who live in the street and those who live in fine houses—that they may one day accept the invitation to join You in the place which Jesus has prepared. Amen.

∽

Larry Crossett is a newspaper correspondent living in Mason City, Illinois, and author of the family-friendly humor column "The Midwest Journey," free via email at larry@midwestjourneyservices.com.

What A Difference A Year Makes

Danni Andrew Scully

My mom was born February 29, 1932. To me she was beautiful and formidable and I wanted to be just like her. Mom could do anything she set her mind to, and she instilled this same belief in me. Her drive for life was infectious. Even a diagnosis of pancreatic cancer and subsequent surgery did not stop this woman, who was bigger than life. As her life began to wane, she required more care than she wanted to admit. The job of care-giving fell to me. A stroke left her unable to speak or swallow properly. The day I entrusted her to the care of a nursing home left me sad as I knew I would never bring her home again. Mom passed from this life on July 31, 2011.

In the weeks following Mom's passing I was in a daze. My world had stopped, and I didn't know what to do with myself. As a writer I hoped I could find solace in my work, but I could not put two coherent words together. One month to the day after my Mom passed away, I received an email telling me I had won a scholarship to a writer's conference. I went to my first CLASS Christians Writers Conference and I knew this was God's way of showing me life wasn't over yet. I learned many things and met amazing people.

Upon returning home I was determined to submit a book proposal and write the book which would grace the top of the New York Times bestseller list. Soon grief and depression returned. I missed my mom terribly and I didn't know how to let go of the waves of grief overtaking me at the worst possible moments.

Each year I would attend yet another writer's conference and each year my resolve to write an award-winning book soon ended as I battled the worst depression of my life. Depression is not new to me as I was diagnosed with Bipolar Disorder in 1995. Yet another loss threatened my life as I broke up with the man I had hoped to marry. Knowing deep in my soul this relationship needed to end, I walked away from the man I had hoped to marry with a heavy heart. Soon I gave up trying to write.

Thanksgiving found me sitting alone in my small apartment. Sobs wracked my body as I lay on the floor. I begged Jesus to help me make some sort of sense out of the mess my life had become. Depression continued to deepen as my life came to a grinding halt. For two long months I sat alone in my apartment, watching old movies and grieving the many losses in my life.

The new year brought a resolution to get up and begin moving again. With the help of a hired hand, slowly I worked to repair the damage to my Mom's home caused by a renter. Deep cleaning and new paint rejuvenated the house and brought a fresh outlook to my own life as I gradually began to live again. Before I could complete the house, a back injury forced me to shut down the project.

As I lay on my stomach in excruciating pain, I contemplated the importance of repairing houses as opposed to following God's calling on my life. I knew in my heart the house needed to go. Laying aside the heavy sentimental ties to my Mom's house, I called a realtor friend and put the house up for sale.

Healing came slowly for my body and slower for my heart, and as summer wound to a close I found myself contemplating what a difference a year makes. In one short year I gave up the man I had hoped to marry, the attachment to my Mom's home, and the drive to write a New York Times bestseller. As I lay these dreams at the foot of the cross, I asked God to lay His plans for my life at my feet. Somehow lying on the floor of my apartment in the midst of my grief, I had found the one true person who would never leave me. My relationship with the Lord was strengthened in amazing ways as I gave up my dreams and allowed Him to take control of my life.

Prayer: Dear Lord, please take the mess of my life and make it one that will glorify you. Amen.

∽

Danni Andrew Scully lives in Northern New Mexico. She is an author, speaker, and artist. Danni's heart lies with those who suffer from Bipolar Disorder and Depression. Danni is also an Area Governor for Toastmasters.

My Very Own Abba

Susan Revels

So, Scott," I said. "Would you consider playing Santa for the kids at the Christmas party? All the other teachers at school think you should." The deaf preschool where I taught was a private school, free to have Christmas celebrations. I needed a Santa. My husband's mouth curled up at the corners as he stood there shaking his head at me.

"Susan, those kids would develop a tic as soon as I'd walk in the door. There may be black santas in other parts of the country, but I've never seen one in Albuquerque."

I could see him mulling it over. Scott's being black and my being Italian brought a blend of traditions to our holidays. "Santa" wasn't a big one. *The Night before Christmas* was fun. Our three- and four-year-olds, Gianina and Cole, loved watching the old Rudolph movie every year. But Mama and Papa were the givers of gifts under the tree.

"Well, I could take the kids to work with me so they could see Santa too," I said. "How many more opportunities will come up like this, to play Santa for your own children and 20 other preschoolers?" It didn't take much convincing to say yes. We decided not to tell our kids about the plan.

The day finally came for Santa's visit. Kids and teachers gathered in the playroom decorated with green-and-red paper chains. You could taste anticipation.

Suddenly there was jingling in the hallway. The teachers oooh-ed and aaah-ed to the kids as the sleigh landed and the reindeer pawed the roof. Children squealed. Cole and Gianina pressed against me. I watched them try to contain their excitement.

Then he was at the door. Santa/Papa dressed in the red suit, black boots, white hair, flowing beard, and gloves to cover his hands. The only part of his brown face that showed was around his eyes and cheeks. "Ho ho ho! Merrrrry Christmas!" he bellowed in his best Santa voice.

Scott wasn't even through the door before Cole bolted from my side. Gianina clutched my shirt. Cole zipped his way around tables and chairs without ever taking his eyes off Santa, until he was standing smack dab in front of him, staring straight up into his face. His eyes wide with wonder, his mouth open with astonishment. With every step Santa took into the room, Cole took one step backward, never averting his gaze, never increasing the distance between them. I didn't move. I didn't want to break the spell. *They don't know it's Scott!*

One by one, each student came up to Santa and sat on his lap. Santa asked what they wanted for Christmas and posed for pictures. Cole hovered close and didn't miss a move. Finally it was Gianina's turn, then Cole's, to sit on Santa's lap. Cole was totally smitten. What did he see with his little-boy eyes? A man in red and black, a fairy tale on the outside, but warm and tender and somehow so familiar on the inside?

After Cole's turn, he came to stand next to me. "Santa looks an awful lot like our Papa!" he said. He was totally serious. I could barely hold back my laughter. It took Cole three days before he asked with a grin, "Papa, was that really you being Santa?"

"Oh yes, that was your very own Papa!" I said.

It is my son's expressions I imagine when people ask how I came to believe. Many people struggle with their sin and guilt when they come to the Lord. Some hesitate, thinking they must clean themselves up before they stand before the Living God. That never even occurred to me. I was driven! *God are you real? I had* to know. I *had* to see. Like my son's astonishment, that was *my* face coming to God! Those were *my* eyes wide with wonder! That was *me* with un-averted gaze! I wanted to eat His Word, look into his eyes, and touch His face.

With every scripture read I asked, "Are you there? Do you see me?" But unlike Santa, God is real. The Majesty of Heaven knows my name. The Creator of all things is here with me. "My sins? Take them all!" Like ripping leeches from skin, I threw them at His feet. As He sat on His throne, He took me in His arms. What did I see with my little-girl eyes? My king, my true Father, clothed in light. Warm and tender and oh-so-familiar. My own Abba! My very own!

Prayer: The Spirit (we) received does not make (us) slaves, so that (we) live in fear again; rather, the Spirit...brought about (our) adoption... And by him we cry, "Abba, Father" (Romans 8:15 NIV). Thank you, Father.

~⑤~

Susan Revels is a teacher of the deaf and principal of a preschool for the deaf in Albuquerque, New Mexico. She lives there with her husband, Scott, her fourteen-year-old daughter, Gianina, and her sixteen-year-old son, Cole.

Useful Until the End

Raelene Searle

It hit like a wrecking ball taking aim at a dilapidated, useless building. The car lurched and jerked, our bodies following the same motions. For a moment, neither of us could comprehend what had happened, but the pain was undeniable.

Chaos ensued as a large white truck shot across the road to my right, up and over a curb. Instantly I realized the cause of the jolt we had just experienced. Then just as quickly, the truck backed down off the curb and sped up the road.

A woman was at my window (the passenger side of the car) asking if I was okay. I cried out, "He's leaving."

"No, he's just pulling over."

"No, he's leaving. Get his license number." As the woman continued trying to calm me down, I kept my eye on the truck and kept arguing that it was leaving the scene. I was right; it disappeared around the corner to the right.

Other people had pulled their cars over to check on us. The police and paramedics arrived. My husband exited the vehicle with no injuries, but I stayed in my seat, focused on the fiery pain in my back. *This cannot be happening—not my back.* I already dealt with chronic pain from a lower back fracture, and now I was fearful that I was facing something more serious—although I could not stop focusing on the fact that the truck had disappeared.

Lights. Questions. Pain. Too many voices all at once. I needed to escape and see if I could still move, but it hurt too much. Finally, I heard what I needed to hear: someone had followed the truck and gotten the license number.

I chose not to go to the hospital. My legs and arms were moving fine, so I opted to go home and rest. I could finally rest, knowing we had what we needed for our insurance to track down the driver and truck that had hit our vehicle. Problems holding the right person responsible for the collision was no longer a concern. Unfortunately, the claim process with the truck driver's insurance was not as easy as anticipated. (Okay, I should not have been surprised!)

For nearly six weeks neither the truck nor the driver could be located. The insurance agent told us that since they could not be found to verify the incident, the insurance would deny our claim. Whoa, that is not how an accident like this is supposed to work.

Questions flooded my mind. Anger arose in my soul. I wrestled with how unfair the system was, especially that while I was trying to recuperate, I was the one having to do the work of getting someone to process my claim. With extreme resistance from those who were supposed to be helping me, my anger turned toward the One who calls Himself our Advocate—Jesus.

Why God had allowed this incident to happen was never a question I struggled to have answered. Why He seemed to abandon me in the midst of the chaos was another matter.

Silly mistakes were the real cause for the delay in my settlement, but none of us knew about them until the end. God could have done something—I was His child, His faithful child, who deserved a break. Already having ridden the medical rollercoaster for years, this one time could easily have been an opportunity for Him to do a miracle. It was an easy case. My medical care was actually quite cut and dried. No doctor had seen any structural damage, only aggravation and inflammation. Additional pain management, beyond my normal daily care, was all I needed.

Nearly a year later, after unnecessary delays, the Lord came through as He always does—In His time. I, on the other hand, wrestled intensely with a strong feeling that maybe I wasn't useful to Him anymore—my usefulness had to be the reason for such a delay. However, as with every other day and every other trial, I see why His delays are always relevant and perfect.

More medical trials still plague me today, but I have learned not to question their cause or to think God is no longer planning to use my life for Him, His work, and His glory. Now I know to look for His plans in that day rather than for a big-ending revealing truth.

Prayer: Heavenly Father, by Your great mercies You have created me for Your glory until the day You take me home. Please remind me daily of this truth and Your perfect love. Amen.

Raelene Searle is a Bible teacher, motivational speaker, author, ministry leader, wife, mother, and grandmother. She lives in Albuquerque, New Mexico, with her husband of 32 years, Chip.

God Knew

Sylvia Sisneros

Before heading to Israel last summer, my husband's co-worker (also our friend) asked her if he could bring her back a bottle of oil. He never thought to ask her what kind of oil, but one would automatically think she was referring to anointing oil since we were traveling to the Holy Land.

A few days into our arrival in Israel we experienced our first shopping trip. Because we wanted to get our personal shopping out of the way, we discovered several choices: perfume oil, olive oil, and anointing oil. We had this conversation: "Surely anointing oil is what she is wanting." But what is she going to do with it?

After looking in several shops with no success, we decided, once we arrived back to the hotel, we would text her. "Are you wanting us to bring you anointing oil, perfume oil, or olive oil?" We never received a response. By now I was feeling frustrated. My husband had had enough, and in one of the gift shops, he reached out for anointing oil and said we will take her this.

A few days after we arrived home, my husband delivered the oil to his co-worker. She thanked him without commenting on the type of oil.

We still weren't sure that it was what she really wanted.

Some weeks later we learned this co-worker was diagnosed with breast cancer. I was shocked and upset when my husband called to give me the news. I immediately called her. The conversation moved in a different way than I expected. She was open to my encouragement and even allowed me share some Scripture verses with her.

The following week at church, still thinking about my friend but trying to focus on the sermon message, I suddenly felt as if someone had hit me on the head. My heart stopped as I heard the voice of the Spirit say, "You bought the anointing oil because she is sick." I couldn't believe it! I finally had the answer to my question—and it wasn't from her. She didn't even know why we'd brought her that specific oil.

The very next evening I received a text from my friend with an update about her surgery. She also wanted to let me know the oil we brought her from Israel was used in a special way: her cousin, who is a minister, had prayed and anointed her with *that* oil.

Tears began to roll down my cheeks as I read her text. I immediately wrote back, telling her we had hoped this gift to her would be perfect— and it was. What joy I had in texting her the details of what had happened to me the night before while at church.

Later that evening, on my way home from work, she called me and I asked her about the text I had sent her while I was in Israel—the one she never responded to. She was still not realizing that I never received her text. "Normally I would have selected the perfume oil, so I don't know why I told you to get the anointing oil." Suddenly she understood what I was saying, and realized I hadn't received her text.

We both were silent for a moment and realized God was the one who gave the answer to both of us.

As the transitions of God's earthly creation can be slow and subtle, moving from summer to fall, its grandest beauty is seen in the way the foliage changes; the vast array of majestic colors melds from light green, to yellow, to orange, and finally to the brown of fallen life. While my friend's life changed in a more dramatic sense, without the process of transition, the work of God's plan for her has not been lost in this season of my life. Through this journey I have witnessed His plans for non-believers, and how that plan can include using me. Who would have thought that a simple shopping trip to bring oil to a friend would have been a part of God's eternal plan?

Prayer: Father God, Creator of the Universe, thank you for choosing us to be a part of your eternal work and for providing the courage and strength to face each day. In your loving and gracious name these things I ask. Amen.

⁓

Sylvia Sisneros lives in Bernalillo, New Mexico, with her husband of 36 years, Ronnie. They have two adult married children and two grandchildren. She is an Office Administrator of a local CPA Firm.

Blue Skies

David Cary

I never expected to be in trouble with the Department of Homeland Security. But, on this rainy Thursday morning, I found myself staring at a letter from the agency in disbelief. My Tennessee driver's license was to be sent in along with my car tags immediately. I was not to drive any vehicle until further notice, and they would send a warrant for my arrest if I did not fully cooperate.

I was scheduled to fly out of Memphis that afternoon on a business trip to St. Louis, Missouri. The thought of being detained while going through the security check was unnerving. As an ordained minister, it might not look good if I was handcuffed and led away. I was feeling like a criminal, and I hadn't committed a serious crime as far as I knew. Well, I could think of one little smear on my otherwise clean rap sheet.

Several weeks earlier I had been pulled over by a policewoman for not wearing my seat belt. When asked to show proof of insurance, I presented an insurance card that was outdated by three days. The officer wrote me a ticket for both offenses and said it was mandatory that I appear in court with the proper insurance papers. Here is where the serious crime occurred: I entered the wrong date on the calendar, and thus, missed the court hearing by four days.

When I called the courts to make restitution, I was told to pay all court costs and send in the proof of insurance. I quickly complied, fully expecting to have my criminal record cleared. Instead, something had seriously gone wrong.

It seemed wise to call Homeland Security and see what could be done. The voice mail message reported many callers ahead of me, but provided an office email address as an alternative contact. The necessary copies were quickly scanned and emailed off with a prayer.

Though my stress level was elevated, I decided to go ahead with my flight to St. Louis. Though I'm sure I had a suspicious look of nervousness, passing through security was eventless.

Seeking some kind of resolution, I made another quick call to Homeland Security while waiting at the gate. After 45 minutes of being on hold, a lady answered the phone and kindly said she would look for the email sent earlier in the day.

As she put me back on hold, an announcement came over the terminal intercom stating my flight to St. Louis had been cancelled. I hustled over to the scheduling desk and began the nerve-racking process of rescheduling a flight. To my dismay, no flights would be available until later that night. I felt like I might be a stroke candidate.

With the phone stuck to my ear, I took a deep breath, shut my eyes and said a belated, simple prayer. "Lord, I'm not sure what to do, but I'm coming to you for some supernatural help."

When I opened my eyes, the scheduling agent was studying me with obvious concern—maybe even a little pity. I asked if she could please take one more look for an earlier flight and she kindly agreed to do so.

Within moments, her face lit up and she told me one seat was left on a plane leaving in five minutes. She pointed to a nearby gate as she handed me a new ticket. As I raced toward the gate, the Homeland Security lady came back on the phone. She cheerfully told me I would soon be cleared of any wrongdoing.

I was feeling much better as I ran down the ramp, showed my ticket to the attendant who was in the process of shutting the door, and promptly led me to my seat, 1A.

That's right. First class!

I chuckled as the plane ascended up into the rain and eventually broke through the clouds. I took a moment and thanked God for His reassuring help. After all, in one short day He had carried me from a dark place of trouble with Homeland Security to flying first class in the sunshine.

The skies seemed extra blue.

James 4:10 might cap this day in my life the best. "Humble yourselves before the Lord, and he will lift you up" (NIV).

Prayer: Lord, thank you for your faithfulness. I want to rely on you more, knowing you care for me. In Christ's name. Amen.

❦

David Cary is a certified life coach who has experience in business, ministry, and psychotherapy. He has written for various publications, hosted a nationwide radio broadcast, and served as a District Superintendent in the Wesleyan Church. David and his wife, Holley, live in the Memphis area. Together they have a blended family of two sons and four daughters.

The God I Thought I Knew

Connie Payne

W e sat in the crowded pew, waiting for the funeral to begin. In the hushed room, I pondered the farming accident that took my husband's family friend too soon. That moment, my purse started blaring *I Heard it Through the Grapevine*. Fumbling for my phone, I shut down Marvin Gaye before he could take another breath, and heard a strange, muffled voice. Lifting the phone to my ear, I whispered, "Hello? Who is this?"

"Your father," the voice said, cracking. I could hear my dad sobbing. Alarmed, I looked at my husband, then rushed out the door to take the call. Barely able to speak, Dad said, "It's your mother. She has cancer."

His words seemed distant. I couldn't process. Our friend lay in the casket on the other side of the brick wall I found myself leaning against. And just weeks ago, we learned Aunt Sandra, my husband's unmarried aunt—who loved our children dearly—had stage-four cancer. *What's going on, God?*

My answers would have to wait. Mom had kidney cancer, already in her lungs, and Dad needed sinus surgery. With four of our six children still at home and my job at the Mission put on hold, I spent months driving Mom, Dad, and Aunt Sandra to doctors and hospitals.

Then, people around us started dying. Without warning, two close friends passed away in the prime of their lives, and we lost three uncles. Before my mother's time came, I stayed awake at night, pleading for her life. *God, please save her. She has much more to give, many more people to bless.*

Then, I watched her die.

God, are you playing us as pawns in this game of life?

After Aunt Sandra's painful death, two more aunts would leave us, and I despised our funeral clothes. Days later, my father started bleeding from his nose. "This happens after sinus surgery," the doctors told us—for months. But, it turned out a red herring. They found his lung cancer too late. He fought valiantly, taking chemo with stubborn hope, and managed to live another eighteen months. With great pleasure, he walked down the aisle at my daughter Rachel's wedding, holding my arm. He had no hair on his head, his skin yellow beyond belief. I'll never forget his smile, his frailty. I'll always cherish that day, with Dad dressed in his best, full of honor and pride.

My grandma would die next, refusing to watch another son leave this world before her. Three months later, Dad passed away peacefully— the twelfth in a line of lost loved ones, lasting four and a half years. This time, I didn't pray for God to save my dad. I didn't think He would.

In the quiet aftermath of death, life settled down like dust after a wagon train. I picked up my Bible with a greediness I'd never known before. Everything in my life hinged on the identity of the God I thought I knew. Looking back, I had many years with Him. In the fourth grade, I accepted Jesus as my Savior. In eighth grade, I vowed to serve Him forever. I knew in my heart Someone above this earth had my number.

But now, I could no longer trust Him.

My search soon became an all-consuming passion to understand God. My question, "Who are you, God?" in truth was an accusation: "Who do You think You are?" I had to find out. For two years, I read the Bible hours a day. Cover to cover, and back again.

Along the way, in my reading, I saw a tenacity in God I hadn't seen before. Throughout the pages of the Bible, I met a God who refused to give up on us. Centuries often passed before He reached down with a judgment or a punishment. Like a father, He hoped to gather His children.

The afflictions that seemed terrible shaped God's people, helping them step out of their selfish desires. They set better priorities, even if for a short time, and appreciated the blessings of a Father in heaven who cared enough to show up, and love them.

In the two years I searched for God, I realized I will never have God's-View-of-All-Things. I will never have perfect wisdom and revelation here on earth. But one thing I found: A cherished, trusted friend that I can count on for everything, who knows exactly what I need to draw closer to Him. He is my All in all things.

Prayer: Dear Father, thank you for leading me through the shadow of death, and helping me see your Sonrise on the other side. Amen.

∽

Connie Payne, an avid reader who loves the Lord with all her heart, longs to use her words to glorify God, like many of her favorite authors have done.

Finding the Courage to Fly

Cynthia Siegfried

When you go through deep waters, I will be with you. When you go through rivers of difficulty, you will not drown. When you walk through the fire of oppression, you will not be burned up—the flames will not consume you (Isaiah: 43:2, TLB).

It's not fair," Campbell whined. "I'm almost six and I want to parasail, too. Why should I have to sit in the boat and watch everyone else fly through the air?"

"We'll have to see when we get there," I explained for the third time. "The brochure says you must be six or older to ride—probably for safety reasons. We wouldn't want you to slide right out of the seat." Watching her eyes fill with tears, I added, "Maybe they'll make an exception, when they see how tall you are."

Because Campbell is our daredevil, tough-as-nails, risk-taking grandchild, we weren't surprised by her eagerness and lack of trepidation. Yet, when the captain of the excursion bent the rule for the very persuasive, freckled-face, "almost six-year old," her momentary elation began to subside.

"Are there sharks around here?" she asked. "I think I'll ride between Jim-Daddy and Daddy," she announced, intently watching the other threesomes set sail from the back of the boat. As she sat firmly ensconced between her dad and grandpa, a small hand resting on each of their legs, I was reminded that even the bravest among us sometimes needs an infusion of courage. The touch of a hand, a "you can do it" from a trusted friend, and a loved one to lean on when danger lies ahead help us step out with confidence.

When I was Campbell's age, I was willing to try anything if my father was holding my hand. "Please, Daddy," I begged at the amusement park. "I want to go on the big roller coaster."

"That's my girl," he replied proudly. "No fraidy-cats in this family."

Climbing in the front car, I nestled in under his arm; he wrapped his leg around my small skinny one, anchoring me to the seat. We chugged up the steep incline with anticipation rather than fear because with Daddy by my side, I was oblivious to any danger.

On vacations, I would venture out into the ocean with Dad's arms as my only life jacket. Never mind that he was the ninety-seven-pound weakling in the Charles Atlas body building ads, who would undoubtedly be washed out to sea like a piece of flotsam by a six-foot wave. "Farther, farther," I shouted, as Mom shouted equally loud, "That's far enough. Bring her back."

Dad is long gone from this earth but those childhood adventures taught me to rely on the One who loves me even more than he did. When a situation strikes fear in my adult heart, I remember that my heavenly Father is my strength and security. More importantly, when Jesus left this earth He didn't leave me alone but gave me His abiding Holy Spirit to encourage and help me until He comes again.

What are you facing today that fills you with fear? Cancer? A financial crisis? A child gone astray? Death? You can rest secure and step out in faith knowing you are under the protective wing of our heavenly father. In the shelter of His wing, you can soar to impossible heights.

Prayer: Dear God, thank you for your Spirit, who encourages and strengthens me in every endeavor, who calms my fears, and walks me through the storm. Amen.

⌁

Cynthia Siegfried is the author of *Cancer Journey: A Caregiver's View from the Passenger Seat* and co-founder of F.A.I.T.H.—Facing an Illness Through Him, a support group for families facing cancer.

God is Not Shocked

Pam Flippin

I don't know when anger and hatred crept into my heart. Identifying it was really hard. Surely, if I were angry, I'd be the first to know! But that's not what happened.

"What's wrong?" my high school teacher (also my pastor) asked, when my countenance suddenly changed from happy to sad. It was rare for me to show my pain, but the grief was extreme that day. I could only stare because I dared not open my mouth. One of my stepsisters had run away from home, and when my parents found her and brought her home, she was severely beaten and tied up outside my bedroom door. I cringed with fear, unable to help her. "Father, please comfort her," I cried. "She doesn't deserve this abuse. The pain is too much to bear."

Life at home had always been difficult, but I often dismissed it and pretended everything was all right. I didn't even think to connect all the dots, but I highly suspected my mother was the cause of my pain. "How could you not know?" you might ask. It's simple: If I had allowed myself to accept the truth, I wouldn't have survived as long.

My mother purposed not to bond with anyone, and her willingness to marry men with children was strictly for monetary gain. Basic needs were denied, and for step kids that included food, deodorant, and friends. She used torturous means to accomplish her goals, and we were trained to look the other way. I caught myself twice hoping she'd die in a plane crash, but I quickly repented of those thoughts and determined never to feel hatred for her again.

Night terrors followed me to college. I feared for my youngest brother's life and was concerned for the five stepsiblings between him and me. I had left them alone with the great oppressor, who daily destroyed another piece of their souls. Suddenly, my grades began to fall as I struggled with thoughts of ending my life.

"What is wrong with me? Why do I feel like this?" I asked myself. Prayer was my only outlet. It wasn't safe to tell anyone. I felt guilty. I didn't know if God was still there or if He had turned His back.

Evidently, the hatred for my mother was redirected. I found this out when my college professor, not knowing how suicidal I was, took me to a Christian counseling center for help because I was obviously distressed. "Your test revealed that you are angry, and you've turned that anger toward yourself," the counselor explained.

What a shock! How could I not know I was angry? And why had I assumed responsibility for my mother's actions?

My mother never valued, esteemed, or approved of me, which is hard to understand. The natural role of a mother is to value her children. I know, because I was blessed to experience this with my own kids. I eventually resolved my anger with the help of a skilled therapist. Painful memories still bring some tears, but I no longer hold myself responsible, and I've forgiven the one who was.

My Heavenly Father never turned His back on me. It's comforting to know He's always accepted me just as I am. He heard every cry, every prayer. And it pleased Him to adopt me as His child, because Jesus had redeemed me with his blood. God's grace is sufficient to cover all my sin.

> Blessed be the God and Father of our Lord Jesus Christ, who hath blessed us with all spiritual blessings in heavenly places in Christ: According as he hath chosen us in him before the foundation of the world, that we should be holy and without blame before him in love: Having predestinated us unto the adoption of children by Jesus Christ to himself, according to the good pleasure of his will, To the praise of the glory of his grace, wherein he hath made us accepted in the beloved. In whom we have redemption through his blood, the forgiveness of sins, according to the riches of his grace (Ephesians 1:3-7 KJV).

Prayer: Father, help me to know your perfect love and your ability to heal in my life. Amen.

Pam Flippin, pam.flippin@hotmail.com, completed her Bachelor of Science degree in Christian Education in 2013. She and her husband, Scott, just celebrated their thirtieth anniversary. They adopted two of their four children.

Yo Blondie!

TraciLynn Davy

Yo, Guera!" Marge, my new neighbor, called across the street to me, commenting on my half purple, half white hair. I'm a hair artist and own a salon, she's a retired 70-year-old woman with a big, toothless smile. She has dentures, but seldom wears them. Our journey of love and friendship had begun; I know the Lord brought us together.

Two years into our relationship, Marge was telling everyone I was her *hita* - that is, her daughter. Marge was a widow; she never had any children. Her parents, aunts, uncles, and eight of her nine siblings had already passed away, and she was at odds with her only surviving brother. Marge shared many stories of her life with me, including how she was there for each one of her family members as they died of either cancer or diabetes. She terribly missed her favorite sister, Mary. Many times when I did or said certain things, Marge would get a big smile and say, "You are just like Mary!"

Another year later, when Marge became ill, off to the hospital we went. She had had a mastectomy 25 years earlier, and after all the poking and prodding and hair loss and shots and Chemo—the cancer was back.

Now it was in the colon with spots on her lung—and more. I assured her I would stand by her in whatever choice she made. "No more!" she said. "No more poking! No more prodding! No more Chemo!" Doctors said she had up to a year to live.

I spent more time at Marge's house over the next ten months. She phoned me often, sometimes fifteen minutes before I needed to be at work. "Mija, I've had an accident; I need you!"

It was God's sufficient grace that helped me lovingly clean her up, clean up the mess, and make her breakfast each day. Soon we needed to rearrange her house to put the hospital bed and kitchen table in the front room, and the front room furniture in the kitchen. My clientele knew about my commitment to Marge and understood why I was late or why I answered my personal phone during their appointments. I was three minutes away for her most urgent needs. I grew so weary, I called my cousin JoJo. She also adored Marge, and gladly came to help. I just needed to take a shower, go to the store, and get some sleep.

Marge's pain worsened; piercing headaches made it evident the cancer had invaded her brain. The hospice nurse informed me Marge needed 24-hour care.

Dear Lord, give me your strength. I'm extremely weary. Where do I go for help? Marge has no family and no money to pay for these nurses. JoJo is already giving all her spare time. God, I need Jesus with some skin on. Please help me, I can't do this alone. In Jesus name, Amen.

I started making calls to cancer centers and organizations. "No, we're sorry. We don't have that type of help to give. Why don't you try such and such."

Repeatedly I received the same message. Every time I opened my mouth to speak, I cried. Finally, after many calls, I came in contact with a group called People Living Through Cancer.

"I just need someone to sit with her," I pleaded with the lady. "I'll take care of all her intimate needs and diabetic shots. If needed, I'm just a phone call and three minutes away."

The very next day I started to receive phone calls. Pastor Mark helped me figure out the scheduling. *Thank you, Father God. Jesus with skin on.*

God always answers right on time; Marge was quickly declining. I added food coloring to the liquid morphine to ensure I gave the proper dose when the alarm went off every 30 minutes around the clock.

I hadn't slept in a few weeks. It was December 31st, and Pastor Kim called to check on us; she knew I wasn't OK. Pastors Kim and Mark joined me to pray over Marge and worship. That evening, my dear Marge left us peacefully to be with her Lord and Savior in Heaven.

2 Corinthians 12:9 gives me encouragement: "...My grace is sufficient for you, for my strength is made perfect in weakness" (NKJV).

Are you being the church by loving your neighbor as yourself?

Prayer: Lord, please help me to *be the church* and love my neighbors right where they are.

❧

TraciLynn Davy is the mother of two, Grammie of three. She owns and designs hair at Lord and Lynn Salon in Albuquerque, New Mexico. She lectures and teaches on all aspects of hair artistry.

Stuck in the Starting Blocks

Mike Wolff

For though by this time you ought to be teachers, you have need again for someone to teach you the elementary principles of the oracles of God, and you have come to need milk and not solid food...Therefore leaving the elementary teaching about the Christ, let us press on to maturity, not laying again a foundation of repentance from dead works and of faith toward God...But, beloved, we are convinced of better things concerning you, and things that accompany salvation...For God is not unjust so as to forget your work and the love which you have shown toward His name, in having ministered and in still ministering to the saints (Hebrews 5:12-6:10 NASB).

Apathy caused the undoing of Adam's kingdom. It is a character flaw his sons have struggled with ever since. Having been given the law, he stood like the proverbial doorstop as Eve was deceived. David's fall did not begin when he slept with Bathsheba, but rather when he stayed behind as other kings went out to war. The disciples did not first abandon Jesus in the garden when confronted by Judas's entourage, but by repeatedly taking their rest when He asked them to be vigilant. If a son of Adam is given an easy way out, he will typically take it. The result will more often than not be the same: the fall of his kingdom. Telling a man he can come as he is to Jesus at the point of conversion serves him well. But that's just the start of the race. To continue with that message afterward, however, will consign him to a lifetime of living in his fallen state—an existence hopelessly mired in the starting blocks of a race he should be running.

Yes, Jesus loves us enough to meet us where we are, but everything He taught and modeled while among us was to be the template for moving on to the place of maturity He desired when He said, "Go make disciples *who observe all* I commanded." Jesus took the challenge He lays before every man: "You shall be perfect, as My heavenly Father is perfect." Jesus knew we would never get there, but He made it the finish line of the race so we would never be satisfied with any lesser standard. Paul put it this way, "But earnestly desire the greater gifts, and I will show you a still more excellent way." Both knew men had been created with a desire to explore, the need to work, and a yearning for "the thrill of victory and the agony of defeat." Modern Christendom is boring men to tears with what the writer of Hebrews would call its "elementary" message of "Come as you are," long after they came as they were. When they couldn't find anything in their faith to fulfill their God-given yearnings, they wandered off in search of counterfeit thrills the world is happy to serve up.

As the passage from Hebrews above reveals, continuing to feed men the milk of "the elementary" evangelical message of repentance and faith after conversion fails to mature them. This same passage gives us the solution to our present dilemma. It instructs us to move them on into "the things that accompany salvation," which are good works, love, and missions. Serving up milk Sunday after Sunday, without equal portions of meat consisting of a requirement to keep the Great Commandment and the Great Commission, and then providing worthy mentors to show them the way, has become a storm perfect for destroying Adam's sons. Evangelism without discipleship is largely responsible for the tragic results of virtually every poll of churchgoers taken over the last 50 years, of whom 90+% have checked out of what should be the great race of the Christian faith. They come as they are, leave as they were, to indulge themselves the rest of the week in the world's delicacies that arouse the passions that withered and died in their temple pews long ago.

Prayer: Lord, please send shepherds to teach and lead the men now languishing in the halls of religion, as you did when You sent Your Son. We've returned to temple worship, and we need the Good Shepherd and true disciples to show us the way once more. I pray, do one of those new things You are so famous for, for as it was then my brothers are now lost within their own house.

∽

Mike Wolff has been actively involved in both traditional and para-church ministries since 1978. He is a speaker, discipleship trainer, and writer currently working with Open Doors Ministries in Denver, Colorado, and is the director of Reconnections Ministries. He lives in Denver with his wife of 33 years, Tammi.

So, Now What?
How Do We Come As We Are?

The writers and editors of this book hope you have enjoyed reading the real stories on its pages. We are imperfect people who have felt the unmistakable hand of God on our lives as He has shaped us, moved us, and provided miracles along the way. Praying you will come as you are, we invite you to grow closer to our Savior who accepts you with unfailing love, exactly the way you are.

This Christian group of CLASS writers and speakers gathered in Autumn 2014 in Albuquerque, New Mexico, to celebrate God's Presence in their lives. Under the capable leadership of CLASS staff Gerry Wakeland, Linda Gilden, Karen Porter, and others, they polished their craft as they designed and completed this book in one week. They offer it to you as a sacrifice to God as well as a testimony of His goodness and grace.

As Mike Wolff explained in the last article, we hope you won't stop at the starting block and never get out of the gate into the race for the finish line with God. We encourage you to move forward, as the writer of Hebrews 12:1-2 says, "throwing off everything that hinders [you] and the sin that so easily entangles, and. . . run with perseverance the race marked out for us" (NIV). Above all, "let us fix our eyes on Jesus, the author and perfecter of our faith" (Hebrews 12:2 NIV) as we run. May you not grow weary, but come to the finish line just as you are, warts and all, knowing the forgiveness of a risen Savior, whose tender eyes show us compassion, mercy, grace, joy, and unending love.

Praise Him that He takes our sins and scars, transforming them in a miraculous way, equipping us with gifts of humility and power, which we can use for Him. Now, get up, go out, God-ready, Just as You Are.

 **CLASSBooks**

CLASSBOOKS is an imprint of CLASSEMINARS, Inc.

Other books by CLASSBOOKS

Out of the Overflow

Transformed

Echos of Mercy

Each One Reach One

Refreshing Wind

CLASSEMINARS, Inc. is the premier trainer of Christian communicators. More than 30,000 men and women have learned speaking and writing skills from CLASS. Thousands have discovered the difference that understanding The Personalities makes in life and ministry.

Visit our website at www.classeminars.org to find an event near you.

Made in the USA
Charleston, SC
14 December 2014